MINDSPLIT

The Psychology of
Multiple Personality and the
Dissociated Self

by the same author

A Textbook of Human Psychology
Imagination and Thinking: a Psychological Analysis
Experience and Behaviour

MINDSPLIT

The Psychology of
Multiple Personality and
the Dissociated Self

PETER McKELLAR

J. M. DENT & SONS LTD
London Melbourne Toronto

First published 1979

© 1979 Peter McKellar

Printed in Great Britain
by Biddles Ltd, Guildford, Surrey
for J. M. Dent & Sons Ltd
Aldine House, Welbeck Street, London

British Library Cataloguing in Publication Data

McKellar, Peter
  Mindsplit.
  1. Dissociation (Psychology)
  I. Title
  154   RC553.D5

ISBN 0-460-04348-X

Contents

Acknowledgements

I am indebted to the following: Robert Guyton and Philip Scaddon for their detailed studies of their own hypnagogic imagery; Professor Alan Horsman for advice on English literature; Professor Basil James for advice on depth psychology; Dr James Moody and Henry Tonn for assistance as hypnotists. My colleagues in the department of psychology at the University of Otago have provided valuable suggestions and criticisms: I would mention especially Peter Bradshaw, Jack Clarkson, and David Marks. The late Enid Blyton provided, in her letters to me, unique introspections on her own autonomous creative thinking. I wish also to thank Dr Henry Murray (Morton Prince's successor); quite apart from his help, I have made considerable use of his theory of personality. Jane Fabre, Janice Galvin, Margaret Gilkison and Carol Hunter have each contributed to the production of this book, and I owe a special debt to my secretary, Isabel Campbell, for her work in preparation of the typescript. I acknowledge the help of my co-authors in previously published papers: Lorna Simpson and, with sadness, the late Dr Amor Ardis. Finally I must thank a patient wife for providing our small daughter to whom this book is dedicated.

Peter McKellar

for little Vicky
may she always retain a
mind of her own

Preface

The central theme of this book is dissociation. Human personality is examined in terms of the functioning of its sub-systems. Cases of dual and multiple personality – dissociation in its extreme forms – will be considered. The most famous of all such cases comes from literature, and enables us to think, on occasion, of the 'Mr Hyde' within. This phenomenon, the Jekyll-Hyde personality, is a matter of fact as well as of fictional literature. Among the classic cases to be discussed are those of Miss Beauchamp, Eve White, Ansel Bourne and Sybil Dorsett. Some of the major researchers in this area, like Morton Prince, have argued that dissociation has its place also in the study of the normal personality. There are many signs that dissociation is returning from its ostracism back into psychology. In particular a leading American psychologist, Ernest Hilgard, has provided some challenging experiments which support such a reinstatement, and also applications to the study of the dissociations of normality.

Attention will be given to 'possession' and other happenings which some have chosen to interpret in occult or supernatural ways. The beliefs of the person affected, of those that study him, and of the larger community are all important. Some, like myself, prefer to remain within the scientific and naturalistic framework: our language is that of dissociation, multiple personality, co-consciousness and mental imagery. Others interpret what seem to be similar phenomena in such terms as 'demonic possession', 'spirit controls', 'mediumistic trances' and 'clairvoyance'. Reincarnationist views have also made their presence felt in this area, and both out-of-the-body experiences and lucid dreams have been interpreted accordingly. In this book I have adopted and retained a naturalistic standpoint, yet it is important to recognize the supernatural view as not merely a matter of sixteenth-century Europe. On the contrary, in Africa, Asia, South America, and even areas of Europe and North America, the alternative concept of 'possession' remains widespread. It is very much part of modern times.

Many have made their attempts to map and label the sub-systems of the normal personality. In ancient times Plato viewed it as a man (rationality), a lion (courage and spirit), and a many-headed monster (passions and appetites). Another of his famous metaphors likened it to a charioteer seeking to guide two powerful horses, the one spirited and noble, the other base and ignoble. Later I shall discuss the contributions of the English Bishop Joseph Butler, who viewed personality as rather like a school, governed by a headmaster (conscience), with two senior prefects (prudence and altruism), and many pupils to control (passions, impulses and desires). Freud, for his part, likened the rational ego to a rider seeking to guide a more powerful horse, and his ego, id and superego comprise probably the best-known relatively recent attempt to map the sub-systems of personality. Of great interest are rebellions of these sub-systems, and their lesser delinquencies when they assume an autonomy of their own that may disturb us. We are familiar with many dreams whose form and content seem strangely foreign – quite unlike our usual thoughts and feelings. Other autonomous imagery may intrude when we are half-awake, as invasions of dreamlife processes. These common occurrences – hypnagogic images – illustrate sub-systems with which I shall be much concerned. Indeed it is difficult to define the minor dissociations of everyday life more lucidly than in words many people have selected to describe their own mental imagery, whether waking, sleeping or hypnagogic.

In summary my theme is this. For certain purposes it is valuable to consider the human personality – normal and abnormal – in terms of sub-systems and their autonomous functioning. The concept of dissociation and, to use Ellenberger's term, a 'polypsychic model' of mental life, merits detailed consideration. This theme will be explored in terms of the abnormal, the seemingly supernatural and – not least important – the psychology of the normal person.

As the form of the body is a composition of various parts, so likewise our inward structure is not simple or uniform but a composition of various passions, appetites, affections, together with rationality . . . The principles in our mind may be contradictory, or checks and allies only, or incentives and assistants to each other.

Joseph Butler

There are times when I recognize that I am made up of several persons and that the person that at the moment has the upper hand will inevitably give place to another.

Somerset Maugham

1
The Dissociated Personality

Groups of ideas, together with their emotional concomitants, may become split off from the main personality ... and continue a separate existence.

Karl Menninger

A young Frenchman was sitting on the terrace of a coffee-house in Northern Africa. The town was Oran, and in the warm Algerian sun he was reading a newspaper. His eye was caught by one of the news items: the sudden disappearance from France of a twenty-nine-year-old clerk, and the mystery of what had become of him. The young clerk was mentioned by name and the Frenchman read it with amazement. 'I am that man!'

This case was reported by its investigator, Pierre Janet, in a series of lectures he gave in 1906 at Harvard Medical School. A sub-system of the young man's personality had taken control and adopted a different identity. Janet (1859–1947) was an important pioneer in the study of these and other forms of dissociation of the personality. His interest was not in the psychotic conditions we know as schizophrenia (sometimes loosely called the 'split mind'), but rather in hypnosis, hysterical forms of neurosis, amnesia and related happenings. In his lectures he explained the strange experience of the Frenchman as a *fugue,* and with supporting examples from his other cases he argued that fugues were not uncommon.

The memory disturbances characteristic of what Janet named the fugue are most interesting to the modern psychologist. In *Memory* (1964), Ian Hunter explains the fugue as one of the possible consequences of fantasy. The build-up of a fantasy way of life establishes a new role, even a new existence for the fantasist; he may step into this new role, and it may take over. In such cases this change in personality is accompanied by amnesia (a loss of all memory of the previous identity), commonly motivated by the wish to withdraw from the problems and frustrations of the previous life. Most characteristic is what I shall call *time discontinuities*, that is amnesia for periods of past time. These time losses may be an affair of minutes, days or months.

Early this century the English psychiatrist Bernard Hart was treating a patient with a history of fugues. The patient's life was marked by a series of memory blanks. Hart found that the lost memories of these amnesic periods could be recovered through hypnosis. During one of his hypnotic treatment sessions some strange events occurred. The patient, who had hitherto been courteous and restrained, burst into a sudden rage. He asserted angrily that he had met Dr Hart only once before, and laughed contemptuously when told that there had been, on the contrary, at least twenty previous interviews. When asked about statements he had made earlier he denied ever having made them. Presently he sat down, complaining of a headache, and in a matter of seconds he returned to his usual personality. This case is known in the research literature as 'John Smith and the One-Fifth Man', since Hart had to explain to his patient that at certain times four fifths of him were on the stage, but at other times only one fifth. After this incident the 'One-Fifth Man' personality reappeared frequently. Hart described it as 'always suspicious and hostile' and with 'an unconcealed aversion to myself'. This one-fifth man had complete amnesia for the John Smith personality. He was amnesic for material elicited in former interviews, and was angry and incredulous when such topics were mentioned. In this case of dual personality, Hart came to assess the one-fifth man as a kind of crystallized resistance to the treatment.

Fugues, with their characteristic time discontinuities, represent one form of dissociation. Dual personality, as in Bernard Hart's case, represents a more elaborate manifestation of the functioning of personality sub-systems. In multiple personality there are more than two such sub-systems. A good illustration, which I shall discuss below, is the case of Sybil (Schreiber 1975), a woman who exhibited no fewer than sixteen such autonomously functioning personality systems.

In considering these relatively rare variations of the human personality, I shall not primarily be concerned with the forms of personality-splitting associated with schizophrenia. Although possibly related, the schizophrenic psychoses comprise a different set of problems. Both dual and multiple personality are distinguished from schizophrenia in psychiatric classification: they belong with hysteria, hypnotism, and certain other phenomena on the frontier between psychology and anthropology, where we encounter alleged 'possession' by evil or benign spirits. It is inevitable, therefore, that we shall concern ourselves not only with the abnormal, but with certain phenomena of the allegedly occult and supernatural. Actual cases will be considered, but I shall refer to certain portraits in imaginative literature which also make their contribution. Robert Louis Stevenson's famous story of *Dr Jekyll and Mr Hyde* will be discussed in the next chapter, along with some other literary case-histories which are of substantial interest to scientific psychology.

Dissociation of the personality has been undeservedly neglected in recent years. An exception is to be found in the work of those who have sought to give a scientific and naturalistic explanation of possession and other seemingly supernatural occurrences. One outstanding example is the work of Rawcliffe on *Illusions and Delusions of the Supernatural and Occult* (1959). In seeking to understand not only 'possession', but also clairvoyance, crystal-gazing, automatic writing, poltergeists and experiences in the séance room, many scientists have found the concept of personality dissociation a useful tool. Among those who have been influential in dissociationist psychology two traditions may be distinguished: these I shall call the tradition of Pierre Janet and the tradition of Morton Prince (1854–1920). On the whole Janet was primarily interested in the abnormal: the psychiatric conditions which concerned him most were those of hysteria and its manifestations. By contrast, Morton Prince (and others like Bernard Hart) applied the concept of dissociation to mental life more generally, both normal and abnormal. My own emphasis will be in this tradition. It is my belief that detailed study of amnesic episodes, time discontinuities, nocturnal somnambulisms, fugues and multiple personality cases may increase our overall understanding of the human personality.

Three selected aspects (there are others) of everyday, 'normal' mental life may help as a bridge to the understanding of rarer and more extreme manifestations of dissociation such as multiple personality:

Roles

The word is a metaphor from the theatre. In daily life too, as Shakespeare reminds us, one man 'plays many parts': within a single day a person may, for example, be both motorist and pedestrian, buyer and seller, employer and employee, friend and enemy. There are many opportunities for conflict of roles and for role ambiguity, and serious problems can arise from even the simplest of the role transitions demanded in our daily lives.

Personality Sub-systems

It has often been recognized that each one of us has a multiplicity of selves. Some psychiatrists, such as Eric Berne, have argued that within each person there are three people: an adult, a parent figure and a child. The poet Walt Whitman said, 'I contain multitudes'. One highly anti-social shadow of man's civilized self may emerge with alcohol – that chemical in which the human conscience is said to be soluble. Bernard Hart chose to write of 'logic-tight compartments', seeing each such component as insulated from the rest of the personality.

Mental Imagery

Freud wrote of dreams as 'something alien arising from

16

another world'. Recently the psychologist E. R. Hilgard has pointed out that, in dreaming, one part of us is 'spectator to the drama which another part of us is staging'. Dreams provide one kind of imagery. In wakefulness also we may be acutely aware of eruptions of visual and other imagery which surprises us and seems strangely foreign to our usual personality. Between wakefulness and sleep some people report a third kind of imagery: vivid upsurges of dream-like images as on a private cinema screen. These experiences – hypnagogic images – are not 'thought up' by the would-be sleeper, but 'happen to' him as something alien to his voluntary control.

The cases I shall study, from life and from literature, may seem bizarre. It may be difficult to achieve empathy (strictly, entry into the mental life of) in some of the cases of multiple personality which I shall describe. Yet the more familiar experiences of a change of roles, an awareness that through alcohol or some other agent our own 'Mr Hyde' has taken over, or the surprise resulting from our own dreams and imagery should assist in bridging the gap. In any case, I shall not confine my discussion to hallucination and other such 'abnormal' occurrences; I shall be dealing with many features of normal everyday life, together with other phenomena to which there is the temptation to give supernatural rather than naturalistic explanations.

'Altered mental states' are today receiving considerable research attention. The art of hypnotism has been a source of fascination for centuries, and in an important recent paper entitled 'Dissociation Revisited' (1973) Hilgard argued that 'hypnosis provides a promising set of phenomena for the study of dissociative processes'. Anton Mesmer's *Discovery of Animal Magnetism* appeared in 1779. Renamed 'hypnotism', and thus shorn of imaginative attributes like magnetism, this altered mental state continued to engage research interest. Investigators included such pioneers of modern experimental psychology as William James (1842–1910) and William McDougall (1871–1938), and also such men of literature as

Charles Dickens and Edgar Allan Poe. Among the scientists there have been some exceedingly tough-minded experimentalists – Clark Hull in the 1930s, for example, and Martin Orne and Xenophon Barber in more recent years. Like the contemporary psychologist Hilgard, many of these investigators have accepted a strong link between hypnosis and the phenomena of dissociation.

An important early centre of study was the Salpêtrière Hospital in Paris, under the directorship of the neurologist Jean Martin Charcot (1825–1893). Charcot had many distinguished pupils, but two are of especial interest here: Sigmund Freud and Pierre Janet. These men contributed to the establishment of two different traditions, embracing different terms and concepts. Freud and the psychoanalytic movement as a whole were not interested primarily in dissociation. Janet, on the other hand, became an enthusiastic investigator of the fugue, mental automatisms, hypnosis and amnesia. Of the fugue, Charcot himself remarked how strange it is that the people concerned 'contrive not to be stopped by the police at the very beginning of their journey'. To this Janet added 'they take railway tickets, they dine and sleep in hotels, they speak to a great number of people . . . they are not recognized as mad' (Janet 1907, p. 60). Janet's young Frenchman, for example, acted quite convincingly in his new personality.

A fugue is a flight in two senses: a flight from one personality system to another, and a wandering far from home for days, even weeks, at a time. In this altered mental state, behaviour is not only normal but also tends to be so unobtrusively. These features are apparent in another, better-known case which William James reported from America in *The Principles of Psychology* (1890).

The Reverend Ansel Bourne had been brought up in the trade of a carpenter. Just before the age of thirty he experienced a sudden conversion, and he became quite widely known as an evangelical preacher. On 17 January 1887 he entered a bank in the town of Providence, Rhode Island, and drew out 551 dollars. He did not return home, and his wife reported him missing to the police. Two months later, on 14 March, a man woke up in a flat in the town of Norristown, Pennsylvania, and in a state of great agitation asked his neighbours where he was. The flat was above a confectioner's shop, which the man – known to his neighbours as Mr A. J. Brown – had rented six weeks previously. In this shop Mr Brown had carried on his trade quietly, without seeming in any way unusual or eccentric. He now declared that he was the Rev. Ansel Bourne, that he knew nothing of shopkeeping, and that the last thing he remembered – it seemed only yesterday – was drawing money out of a bank in Providence. He would not believe that two months had passed. During this time he had, as Mr A. J. Brown, been quiet and orderly in his habits. He had replenished his stock of goods from time to time, had cooked for himself in the back of the shop and had attended church regularly. Relatives were sent over from Providence to Norristown to help sort things out: the Rev. Ansel Bourne, as he now was, was brought back to his home with complete amnesia for the events of the Mr Brown personality.

In 1890 William James had the opportunity to conduct an investigation. He and his colleagues decided to use hypnotism. When the Rev. Bourne was hypnotized the Brown personality re-emerged; he had complete amnesia for the Rev. Bourne and when confronted with Mrs Bourne reacted to her as a stranger. When asked about the Rev. Bourne, Mr Brown declared that he had heard of him but had never met him! The investigation revealed a similar amnesia on the part of Bourne for the Brown personality. Yet neither of these personalities had behaved in any way that aroused the suspicion or curiosity of the outside world.

The experiences of the Rev. Bourne lie somewhere between the fugue and the expression of a fully developed multiple personality. In certain circumstances (depending on the prevailing set of religious or psychological beliefs) such a case might have been, and might still be, given a supernatural or

occult interpretation. Certainly, the earliest records of dissociative phenomena are to be found in occult and supernatural literature.

The alternative standpoint of naturalistic science began to
appear with the case of Mary Reynolds, which was first
described in 1817. Original details of the case were provided by
Professor Andres Ellicott, a relative of the patient. Mary was
born in England but raised in Philadelphia from the age of
four. The daughter of a prominent Baptist, she was reared in a
strictly religious environment into which she brought additional devotions and meditations of her own. Until the age of
eighteen she appeared 'normal', but she then developed 'fits'
which left her blind and deaf for four to five weeks. These lesser
dissociative occurrences were followed by more dramatic ones.
After some months she went into a deep sleep lasting nearly
twenty hours. From this she awoke wholly unaware of her
surroundings. The case aroused the interest of William
McDougall some hundred years later. In his *Outline of Abnormal
Psychology* (1926) he said this of Mary's new state: 'as far as all
acquired knowledge was concerned, her condition was precisely that of a new-born infant'. (This was a slight exagger-
ation: she could, in fact, pronounce a few words.) In this
'second state' Mary learned rapidly, and she regained her
abilities to read, write and calculate. The 'second state' personality was buoyant, witty and fond of nature, but amnesic for
the 'first state'. After another five weeks, Mary fell into another
long, deep sleep, from which she awoke in her 'first state'. The
two personalities alternated. They were mutually amnesic,
except that in the 'second state' Mary would sometimes have
dim and dreamlike memories of herself in the primary state. As
time went on the second state gained over the first; finally it
became permanent until Mary's death in 1854. Janet was later
to write of 'dominating somnambulisms', and many of the later
cases of dual and multiple personality have shown a similar
outcome. The two sub-systems seemed also to differ in age, the
second state being more youthful than the first; this feature too

has appeared in later reported cases of multiple personality.

Instances of dual and multiple personality have been reported from time to time ever since this early case. In 1944 Taylor and Martin surveyed the existing research literature. They set out as sceptics but their study convinced them of the reality of the phenomenon. Their own definition is of 'two or more personalities, each of which is so well developed and integrated as to have a relatively coordinated, rich, unified and stable life of its own'. Three of the most famous cases may be mentioned: Christine Beauchamp (studied by Morton Prince), Eve, with her sub-personalities Eve White and Eve Black (studied by Thigpen and Cleckley), and the more recent case of Sybil Dorsett. Sybil, with her sixteen sub-personalities, represents a useful bridge between Freud and the psychoanalysts on the one hand, and the dissociationist tradition of Pierre Janet, William James, Morton Prince, William McDougall and Bernard Hart on the other. An unusually interesting case of multiple personality, Sybil was given detailed treatment by a qualified psychoanalyst.

With these illustrative cases in mind, I shall attempt an examination of dissociative phenomena in all their variety. Adopting the method of the naturalist I shall be concerned first with description and classification, and only then, as far as possible, with explanation. Using a simple classification of my own I shall discuss four types of mental automatism, which I have taken as reference points on a continuum. In tracing this continuum I shall make use of some distinctions to be found in the early work of Pierre Janet, even though these differ somewhat from current usage. For example, Janet does not identify somnambulism with sleepwalking. Instead he distinguishes *nocturnal* somnambulism as a special case of a broader phenomenon. Somnambulism may also occur in the waking state and may be distinguished from fugues on the one hand and multiple personality on the other. To take an example, a psychologist colleague reports the following instance which he himself observed. While he was in a room talking to a forty-year-old woman, she suddenly became anxious, and very angry. Then her head went down, and after a period of silence a childlike voice began to speak. In this voice the woman relived events when, as a twelve-year-old, she had first learned that her father had died. Her parents had kept it from her, but she knew it all the same. She had run to the beach, and now, in the voice of that twelve-year-old girl, she was pleading again with her father not to die. The somnambulism lasted for a period of about ten to fifteen minutes, after which she collapsed. On being put to bed she slept for an hour, and after waking she had amnesia for these childhood events she had re-enacted. When she woke up she was puzzled. She wanted to know what she was doing there in bed, and what had happened in the period of time she had lost. Briefer dissociative episodes of this kind may be contrasted with the more elaborate ones seen in the fugue and in multiple personality.

Using as a basis Janet's pioneer work, I have distinguished four types of automatism:

Type-1 Automatisms

We are familiar with these in everyday life. They are closely associated with well-practised or 'overlearned' activities such as typewriting, car driving and piano playing. An experienced driver is able to talk and think while driving and a skilled typist or piano player may be able to carry on a conversion at the same time as performing. Answers to simple calculations come to us automatically, from mathematical tables we have over-learned, and we are able to sign our names without having to think out what to do. Without these type-1 automatic actions everyday living would be hard work.

Type-2 Automatisms

These occurrences are called by Janet *monoideic* somnambulisms. They may occur spontaneously, as when a person relives an emotionally important past event in a brief episode involving an altered mental state. One of Janet's patients, Irénè, had bursts of somnambulism during which she would re-enact the distressing events connected with the death of her mother, whom she had nursed faithfully. Somnambulisms may also be produced artificially in the hypnotic state. Post-hypnotic suggestion in its simplest form, e.g. 'when I take out my handkerchief you will go to the door and turn the knob', is one example. The hypnotized person is given amnesia for the suggestion, but on being awakened – although unaware of the instruction – he performs the required act when the signal is given. We also encounter nocturnal somnambulisms; sleepwalking (the incidence in one American study was as high as 5 per cent of children) is the best-known example. Some nocturnal somnambulisms are of a more elaborate kind, and may involve walking, talking and enacting some past event: in this respect they lie part way between type-2 and type-3 automatisms.

Type-3 Automatisms
These are more complex (Janet calls them *polyideic*). They are the fugues, and are characterized by a multiplicity of ideas. Janet's young Frenchman and the Rev. Ansel Bourne illustrate this type. A type-3 person is much less likely than a type-2 to attract attention to himself. In his new role he puts on a sufficiently expert performance to avoid the curiosity of others. As in type-2 automatisms there is amnesia for the normal state of consciousness.

Type-4 Automatisms
These are more complex still. They embrace the rare cases of dual and multiple personality. Nemiah (1975) refers to two hundred such cases in the research literature. Best known among them are Morton Prince's Christine Beauchamp and the 'three faces' of Eve, with her sub-personalities Eve White, Eve Black and Jane. Earlier than either of these, Pierre Janet reported the case of 'Félida X'. In her 'no. 1' personality, Félida was reserved, depressed and timid, with many bodily ailments. When her 'no. 2' personality took over she would be

active, gay and in excellent health. The co-existence of these two personalities within the same body had some awkward consequences. During one visit she paid to her original investigator, Dr Azim, Félida in her 'no. 1' state consulted him about some puzzling recent disturbances in her health. Then the 'no. 2' personality took over, and laughingly apologized for troubling him. The 'no. 2' personality knew something that Azim had in the meanwhile diagnosed and was wondering how to break it to the 'no. 1' personality, who had amnesia for the relevant events. Félida was pregnant.

In many cases of multiple personality we encounter this same difference between a depleted and depressed personality on the one hand, and a gay and vivacious secondary personality on the other. Frequently the friends the one makes are uncongenial to the other, and some acute social and personal problems can arise. In the Eve case, 'Miss Eve Black' (who always retained her maiden name) found the husband of 'Mrs Eve White' thoroughly objectionable, and she had a dislike verging on hatred for Eve White's child. I have some understanding of these problems from personal experience. Years ago I knew one, but not both, of a pair of female identical twins. The uncomfortable experience of being 'cut dead' in the street by someone one thinks one knows well has an uncanny resemblance to the embarrassments reported by friends of one of the sub-systems of a multiple personality. Many examples of this sort of confusion are to be found in the social relationships of the sixteen sub-personalities of Sybil Dorsett.

My four types are only reference points and finer gradations could be drawn. In transitions from type-1 to type-2 we find many interesting phenomena: automatic writing, crystal-gazing, personified systems of imagery and variants of the fantasies of sleep such as 'lucid dreams'. While they are wholly compatible with good mental health they represent a bridge to more extreme dissociations of types 2, 3 and 4. Eruptions of autonomous mental imagery have often been reported in the lives of writers, painters and other artists. These literary and artistic aspects of the more minor manifestations of dissociation will be considered more fully in later chapters, but we shall look briefly here at some illustrations.

In her waking mental life Enid Blyton, the children's writer, received much help from a dissociated system of autonomous imagery which she labelled her 'undermind'. Over a number of years she told me in a fascinating series of letters how her undermind, with its 'private cinema screen', would compose the stories for her. Her biographer (Stoney 1974) reveals that in later life these autonomous images took over, resulting in an invasion of consciousness which seriously interrupted her normal mental health.

The imagery of dreams and nightmares seems to have contributed substantially to the Gothic school of horror novels. Horace Walpole, for example, dreamed of a huge hand in armour on the banister of a staircase in an ancient castle: he awoke to write *The Castle of Otranto*. As we shall see in the next chapter, the tale of *Dr Jekyll and Mr Hyde* had a somewhat similar origin in a nightmare. Stevenson made regular use of dream material, and both Charles Lamb and Thomas de Quincey are known to have used hypnagogic imagery as source materials. Of particular interest is an account in Emily Brontë's *Wuthering Heights* of a visual hypnagogic image. The narrator tells how just before sleep he had read the name 'Catherine'. When he settled down to sleep, 'a glare of white letters started from the dark, as vivid as spectres the air swarmed with Catherines'. Emily's sister, Charlotte, in Chapter 38 of her novel *Villette*, relates how Lady Snow is given a drug to ease her pain, and afterwards wanders through the streets of the town. The town is one blaze, 'one broad illumination . . . it is a strange scene, stranger than dreams'. Charlotte Brontë declared that she had never taken opium, but her friend Mrs Gaskell (who knew opium well) wrote that the description was 'exactly like what I had experienced' (Hayter 1968). What Charlotte Brontë did say was that she sometimes made use of her hypnagogic experiences, and it is my suspicion that she did so here.

The use of chemicals to increase imagery has a long and colourful history. My own research interest in psychopharmacology has focused on hallucinogenic drugs, in particular mescaline. Many investigators have noted independently the strong resemblances between hypnagogic and hallucinogen-induced mental imagery. It has also been established that various hallucinogens, such as mescaline, lysergic acid diethylamide and psilocybin, produce remarkably similar imagery. The altered mental states and dissociative phenomena produced by these drugs are of great scientific interest. Five groups of phenomena, all readily produced in hallucinogen experiments, may be kept in mind in our consideration of dissociated systems, their phenomena, their classification and their mechanisms:

Autonomous Visual Imagery. Such images appear to come from some system of the personality alien to the self.

Time Discontinuities. These bear some resemblance to those of type-2, type-3 and type-4 automatisms. Much can be lost in these amnesic periods, and the results can be alarming. People may suddenly appear in different parts of the room, for example, rather than be seen to be moving continuously around it.

Body-image Changes. These are quite common, particularly in the hypnagogic state. Each of us has an impression of his or her own body as an object in space with spatially related parts. This body-image may change; its growing or shrinking was likened by several of our subjects to the experiences of Alice in Wonderland after eating the mushroom. In multiple-personality cases the various sub-systems may have different body-images: this was strikingly the case with Sybil Dorsett.

Dissociated Emotions. It is not that the perceptual stimuli or hallucinations evoke depression, elation or some other emotion; these emotions occur, erupt, of their own accord. The subject seeks to rationalize them in terms of the perceptions or hallucinations he happens to be having.

Hallucination. The hallucinogens mainly evoke visual rather than auditory hallucinations. Aspects of one's own mental life are projected into the outside world, and appear to be 'out there' rather than within.

In 1967, when Henry Tonn and I were reporting a hypnotic experiment of our own, we argued for a reconsideration of dissociation as a concept in psychological theory. We wrote, 'Need we insist on regarding dissociation as an all or nothing phenomenon? Are there not *degrees of dissociation?*' For the most part the human personality functions as an organized whole; its sub-systems are integrated. But there are exceptions.

In his Presidential address to the Medical Section of the British Psychological Society in 1939, Bernard Hart commented regretfully upon the quite remarkable neglect of dissociative phenomena. This was in part due to the enormous influence of Freud and the psychoanalytic movement. Freud had studied the hysterical neuroses, and the uses of hypnosis in the investigation of them, in Paris under Charcot. Later he had also studied at the rival school of Liébault and Bernheim in Nancy, which also used hypnotism. But for a number of reasons he had abandoned this technique in favour of other methods. The dissociationist tradition has indeed long been overshadowed by Freud, but there are signs of a revival of interest amongst psychologists, notably E. R. Hilgard. It is time that we examined more carefully the contribution that the dissociationists – particularly Janet, Prince, James, Hart and McDougall – can make to our understanding of the human personality.

In this book I shall be dealing with the findings of psychology and with true stories of dissociative behaviour – from the startling case of Sybil Dorsett with her sixteen personalities, to more common phenomena of normal mental life – but I wish also to draw attention to the considerable insights of some literary men and women. Quite apart from the mysteries of literary inspiration (we shall have more to say about the influence of dream-imagery, drugs and personal experience in the lives of writers and other artists), the very process of creating convincing fictional characters involves careful observation of human nature, and there are many descriptions of mental disturbance in literature that we would do well to study.

From time to time, writers introduce into their dramas a character whom I have chosen to call the Psychologist in literature. In Ibsen's *The Wild Duck,* for example, the materialistic physician Dr Relling adopts a psychological standpoint throughout: he becomes the mouthpiece for Ibsen's own profound insight into the darker aspects of human motivation, where unconscious malice can underlie the activities of a sentimentalist. In *Brand,* Ibsen uses a similar character to reveal the destructive impulses behind the fanatical puritanism of Pastor Brand. This is not so very far from Freud's later pronouncement that in disorders of the human conscience 'what holds sway is a pure culture of the death instincts'.

Creative writers have long analysed human motives. From the ancient Greek tragedies through Shakespeare to the modern 'psychological' novel, world literature provides us with countless acute and useful portraits of ourselves. My selection is a personal one and I have concentrated on descriptions of what seem to be clear cases of dissociation, rather than on, say, conflicting loyalties or self-deception. In this field, the Russian novelist Dostoyevsky has made a major contribution. Himself an epileptic, he had a profound understanding of the altered mental states which that illness can produce. In *The Possessed* he applies the notion of demonic possession to the study of disruptive groups attempting to overthrow the authoritarian rule of the Tsars. In *The Brothers Karamazov* the conflict between good and evil *within the same man* forms a central theme. In this novel, dissociation, hallucination and the malevolent alter ego are given detailed and penetrating analysis.

Stevenson's horror-story, *Dr Jekyll and Mr Hyde*, is another seminal example. Stevenson (1850–1894) corresponded regularly with Henry James, the novelist brother of William James the psychologist, who himself contributed substantially to the study of dissociation. In Morton Prince's opinion, 'Stevenson, in his imaginative creation . . . anticipated the discoveries of psychological research'. In the chapter following we shall look in more detail at several such anticipations in creative literature.

2
The Jekyll and Hyde Syndrome

*I stood already committed to a profound duplicity of life . . .
both sides of me were in dead earnest . . .*

Dr Jekyll

Robert Louis Stevenson's *Strange Case of Dr Jekyll and Mr Hyde*
(1886) is the most famous case so far of dual personality and it
is of great interest to investigators of dissociation. The sub-
stance of the story was produced in Stevenson's mind through
a nightmare, during which he screamed out so loudly that his
wife woke him. 'I was dreaming a fine bogey tale', he said
reproachfully.

This particular set of dream images had come to someone
with a mind well prepared for such invasions, an author who
habitually made use of his own autonomous thought-
processes. In 1892 Stevenson stated that he was 'from a child
an ardent and uncomfortable dreamer'. Writing of himself in
the third person he records that at some point he began 'to
dream in sequence, and thus to lead a double life – one of the
day – one of the night'. He proceeded to turn this to account
and 'when he lay down to prepare himself for sleep, he no
longer sought amusement, but printable and profitable tales'.
Enid Blyton spoke of her 'undermind' as the source of her
'private cinema screen'. Stevenson spoke of his 'little people',
who would 'labour all night long' and work on his behalf at
'making stories for the market'. In the case of *Dr Jekyll and Mr
Hyde* he had spent two days consciously racking his brains for a
plot. Then 'on the second night I dreamed the scene at the
window, and a scene . . . in which Hyde, pursued for some
crime, took the powder and underwent the change in the
presence of his pursuers. All the rest was made awake, and
consciously . . .'

In Stevenson's story there is a sharp conflict between good and evil, between the virtuous Dr Jekyll and the malevolent Mr Hyde. Hyde was possessed of a violent hatred of Jekyll, which he found various ways of expressing: for example, by automatic writing: Jekyll reports him as 'scrawling in my own hand blasphemies on the pages of my books'. Conflict, mutual hatred and automatic writing have featured in many of the factual cases of personality dissociation, as we shall see.

Some of Stevenson's earlier emotional preoccupations are revealing. In 1879 he had published, with W. E. Henley, a play entitled *Deacon Brodie, or the double life*, which was first performed in Bradford in 1882. Its theme was 'the day versus the night', the evil that lies behind the face of goodness in man. The play was based on fact, on the life of a certain William Brodie – by day a respectable craftsman and by night the leader of a gang of thieves. The historical Brodie was a friend and companion of Robert Burns (the title 'Deacon' was awarded to him as head of a guild) and was hanged for his crimes in Edinburgh in 1788. In the play, Brodie bolts the door, changes his coat and declares 'by night we are our naked selves . . . the day for them, the night for me'. Stevenson had been reared on the story of Brodie. His childhood nurse, Alison Cunningham, a Calvinist, inspired in him a fear of the Devil and Hell: she regaled him with stories of Brodie, and often took him to see Brodie's Close in Edinburgh, a narrow alley of the old town. Stevenson wrote the first version of his play on Brodie when he was only fourteen.

Between the published Brodie play and *Dr Jekyll and Mr Hyde* we also encounter Stevenson's frightening short story, *Markheim* (1885). Markheim the thief kills for profit, then hallucinates and talks with the devil. Sir Sidney Colvin, who knew Stevenson well, talked of 'the dialogue of Markheim with his other self'. This theme of the guilt-obsessed man, confronted with a personified evil which is often simply his rejected self, has a long tradition. It lies at the heart of the Faust legend, for example. In the mediaeval period in general, the Prince of

Darkness was a very real figure and temptations were often personified as evil spirits. One of Luther's biographers (Friedenthal) records that for hermits and desert monks in the fifteenth and sixteenth centuries, 'demons and the devil in many guises' were their sole companions; he adds that their uncompromising asceticism offered no protection against personified temptation. Such belief in 'possession' or persecution by evil spirits is by no means confined to the Middle Ages, as we shall see.

In contrast to this demonological approach, it was Carl Jung (1875–1961) who proposed the notion of the *shadow* of the conscious self. He described the shadow as the 'repressed aspects of the personality', which might sometimes (but by no means always) be the source and explanation of the dissociated person's 'other selves'. In *The Brothers Karamazov* (1880) we find Dostoevsky exploring the same theme; he gives a detailed account for the 'brain fever' of Ivan Karamazov who, like Stevenson's Markheim, hallucinates his own malevolent 'shadow'. It too takes the form of the Devil, whom Ivan sees and with whom he speaks. Ivan talks of this to his brother: 'He is myself, Alyosha. All that's base in me, all that is mean and contemptible . . .' Dostoevsky even takes into account the possibility of hereditary influences in dissociative conditions, referring to Ivan's mother Sofya as one who 'fell into that kind of nervous disease which is most frequently found in peasant women who are said to be "possessed by devils" '.

Like Stevenson, Dostoevksy anticipated himself. An earlier short story published in 1846, *The Double*, bears the same relation to Ivan's dissociation as does the Brodie play to *Dr Jekyll and Mr Hyde*. Dostoevsky's biographer Grossmann describes *The Double* as 'a psychological story in depth of a split personality' (Grossmann 1974). Of especial interest is Dostoevsky's own comment on the apparent failure of his earlier short story: 'Why should I forfeit an excellent idea, a character type of supreme social importance, which I was the first to discover and which I heralded?' (cited in Grossmann 1974).

If we leave behind us the pre-scientific forms of demonology and the Faust legend, we seem to be coming closer to the origins of the concept of dual personality, at least in literature. Dostoevsky's short story relates the oddities in the mental life of Mr Golyadkin, who meets and befriends Mr Golyadkin *junior*. In an atmosphere heavy with a sense of persecution, and aware of strange discontinuities in the passage of time, the unhappy man argues and pleads with his double. Eventually this double assumes control of his personality and takes over his life. He is overwhelmed by his stronger alter ego. This closely resembles the factual case of Mary Reynolds, and the 'dominant somnambulism' about which Janet was later to write. The phenomenon of hallucinating oneself – *autoscopic hallucination* – is, like multiple personality, a rarity. A naturalistic interpretation of the story would say that autoscopic hallucination figured prominently in the incipient breakdown which was to engulf the wretched Golyadkin.

Some of the raw materials of the story can doubtless be found in the altered mental states of Dostoevsky's own epileptic personality. Elsewhere, for example in *The Idiot*, he gives intimate and penetrating descriptions of such personality changes. He was on most friendly terms with his own physician, Dr Stepan Yanovsky, and frequently borrowed books from him. Yanovsky reported that these were 'especially books dealing with diseases of the brain, the nervous system and mental illness'. Although *The Double*, like Stevenson's Brodie play, was not a success, Dostoevksy did not forget this character type – as we shall see from a closer look at the story of Ivan Karamazov.

The plot of *The Brothers Karamazov* centres on the murder of their hated father by one of four brothers. Dmetri, who though innocent, is tried for the crime. At the trial Ivan seeks to intervene in his brother's defence; but his testimony is ineffective, not least because of his 'brain fever'. He seeks to bring into the courtroom as a confirmatory witness the product of his own hallucination, the Devil. Many brilliant professionals – Janet, Morton Prince, Eugene Bleuler – have studied and written about dissociation, but they are hard put to it to match the insights of Dostoevsky here. It is a measure of the author's understanding of dissociation that Ivan is aware from time to time that the Devil he sees and hears is a part of himself. Although Dostoevsky maintains a naturalistic standpoint, there is a passing allusion to demonology here too. Ivan at one point snatches up a glass and throws it at the Devil, who remarks: 'he remembers Luther's inkstand'. This refers to an old story that Luther had once thrown an inkstand at a hallucinatory Devil of his own. Profound conflict troubles Ivan Karamazov as much as it did the historical Luther before him. Ivan is very much aware of the possibilities of human evil, including evil in himself. Earlier he has expressed the view that if the Devil does not exist then man has created him, in his own image and likeness. In a moment of insight he cries out to the hallucinatory figure: 'For it's I, I myself speaking, not you . . . you are a lie, you are my illness . . . you are my hallucination. You are the incarnation of myself, but only one side of me . . . of my thoughts and feelings, but only the nastiest and stupidest of them . . .'

Dissociation cannot simply be equated with repression; it involves something more. The conflict is dealt with not merely by forgetting, but by a splitting off of sub-systems which then operate as foreign bodies within the personality. As Ivan's insights show repression of memories and impulses may contribute to these sub-systems: he recognizes 'all my stupid ideas, outgrown, thrashed out long ago, and flung aside like a dead carcass, presented to me as something new'. The philosopher Nietzsche, who described Dostoevsky as 'the only psychologist from whom I have anything to learn', has a most appropriate formula: ' "I did it," says memory. "I did not do it," says pride. Eventually memory yields.' The relation of repression, and the subsequent autonomous functioning of the repressed material, to dissociation is expressed by Dostoevsky in one incident in particular where the Devil tells Ivan a story about a man sentenced to walk a quadrillon miles. Ivan recognizes this as a short story he had written himself years earlier at the age of seventeen at high school – a story he had forgotten. So his own imagination and memories had produced the Devil. Triumphantly he declares that now he has positive proof: 'You are a dream, not a living creature.'

The intensity of Ivan's mental conflict and the violence of his rejection of his alter ego (like Jekyll's rejection of Mr Hyde) are vividly portrayed by Dostoevsky, and the descriptions bear a marked resemblance to subsequent cases of multiple personality reported from life. Ivan's passionate hatred of the hallucinatory figure – this sub-system of himself – is prominent throughout the book. He remarks with feeling to his brother Alyosha, 'I should be awfully glad to think that it was *he* and not *I*.' Conflict divides him from himself and he represses what he most hates in himself. He projects that hated self, and he

LITERARY CHRONOLOGY

1839	Poe: *William Wilson*
1846	Dostoevsky: *The Double*
1849	Melville: *Mardi*
1868	Collins: *The Moonstone*
1879	Dostoevsky: *The Brothers Karamazov*
	Stevenson & Henley: *Deacon Brodie*
1885	Stevenson: *Markheim*
1886	Stevenson: *The Strange Case of Dr Jekyll & Mr Hyde*

hallucinates. Ivan is portrayed as a quite merciless investigator of his own dissociation, struggling to the bitter end with the conflicting ideas of 'beyond good and evil' that were later to obsess Nietzsche. His insights into dissociation, hallucination and the divided personality merit detailed examination. There was much of his author in Ivan Karamazov, and like Dostoevsky himself Ivan clung wholeheartedly to a naturalistic interpretation of dissociation.

We move now from Russia back to England, and to the long friendship between Charles Dickens – with his intense interest in 'mesmerism' and its associated trance states – and Wilkie Collins. Wilkie Collins was interested in somnambulistic behaviour. His novel *The Moonstone*, published in 1868, appeared two years after Dostoevsky's *Crime and Punishment*. In the Wilkie Collins novel the whole plot depends on the different behaviour of a man in an altered mental state. A gem stone has disappeared, believed stolen. As the story develops it emerges that it has been taken by Franklin Blake in a somnambulistic state induced by laudanum (tincture of opium) administered to him without his knowledge. In normal wakefulness he has total amnesia for this action, but when laudanum is again administered to him he repeats his former actions. This phenomenon is well known to modern experimental psychology under the label of *state dependency*. It is interesting that these processes are uncovered in the story by a character who is familiar with the writings of one Dr Elliotson, who was a pioneer of the use of hypnotic methods in controlling pain during surgical operations, and the instructor of Collins's friend Charles Dickens in hypnotism. The passage quoted in *The Moonstone* from Elliotson's writings concerned 'an Irish porter . . . who forgot, when sober, what he had done when drunk; but, being drunk, again recollected the transactions of his former state of intoxication'.

This is the earliest reference I know of in literature to a case of 'state dependency', and I am indebted to a psychologist colleague for drawing my attention to it. I am further indebted to the same colleague for a personal illustration of state dependency. One evening he was attending a convivial party. He was called away from this to his university department, where he met some of his students. The following day he was unable to remember why he had visited the department that night, or which students he had seen there. On that next day it happened that he was talking with a research worker who was studying the effects of alcohol on memory. The two of them

The Jekyll and Hyde Syndrome

discussed state dependency, and the lecturer's amnesic problem. The researcher then found a solution. He took the lecturer up to his laboratory and gave him a good drink of the vodka he was using in his experiments. The lecturer now found that he was able to recall both why he had visited the department the previous night and which students he had seen there. The accuracy of his recall was verified independently with the students concerned.

Fischer (in Segal and West 1975) draws attention to a comparable incident in the classic Charlie Chaplin film, *City Lights*. Chaplin comes to the rescue of a drunken millionaire who is trying to commit suicide. In gratitude the man takes him home and rewards him with food and luxuries. But next morning the millionaire has sobered up, and he has amnesia for the whole matter. He has no idea who the little tramp is and has him thrown out by the butler. Soon afterwards the millionaire is drunk again: in this altered mental state he recognizes the little tramp and befriends him once more. And so the saga continues: befriended, thrown out, befriended, thrown out, etc. In his discussion of this incident, and of state dependency in general, Ronald Fischer cites experimental findings. In one experiment (representative of many) the subjects memorized material under the influence of alcohol. When sober they exhibited diminished recall. Given alcohol again, their memory performance improved to a statistically significant degree. The phenomenon of state dependency was clearly recognized by Wilkie Collins, probably from his knowledge of the work of Elliotson on hypnotic somnambulisms. The amnesic barrier involved resembles the kind of amnesia we find in posthypnotic suggestion. Under the heading of 'state dependency', these dissociative phenomena are today receiving considerable attention in the psychological laboratory. As so often, literature anticipated the work of the scientist.

American literature has also made its contributions. Two illustrations may be taken from such writings to illustrate an understanding of the sub-systems of the human personality.

There is a short story by Edgar Allan Poe (1809–1849) entitled *William Wilson* and published in 1839, the theme of which bears a strong resemblance to Dostoevsky's *The Double*. In the American story, which pre-dates the Russian, a certain William Wilson encounters his double: the man has the same name, same height and same birth date and he speaks in a voice 'the very echo of my own'. Like Dostoevsky's Golyadkin, Wilson is persecuted by this obsessive alter ego, towards which he reacts with extreme hatred; and there are similar indications of what Pierre Janet was later to call a dominant somnambulism, a takeover by the secondary personality. In Poe's story this is averted by an act of murder.

Another example from American literature describes a rather more benign form of dissociation and automatism than those we have been discussing. Herman Melville (1819–1891) is best known for his story of Captain Ahab's obsessive-compulsive pursuit of the white whale, *Moby Dick* (1851). But three decades before *Dr Jekyll and Mr Hyde* an earlier story of his contains a clear case of dissociation. In *Madi. and a Voyage Thither*, the chattering philosopher, Babbalanje, is from time to time interrupted by a 'mysterious indweller' who is 'locked up' inside him. In many respects this secondary personality, Azzageddi, anticipates Stevenson's Mr Hyde and Ivan Karamazov's hallucinatory Devil.

I have already referred to 'the Psychologist' in literature – the fictional character who becomes a vehicle for the author's own psychological insights. Melville himself says that an author may say or insinuate 'the things which we feel to be so terrifically true that it were all but madness' for others to say or even hint at them. Babbalanje is a lesser psychologist than Ivan Karamazov; in fact the philosopher is portrayed, as his name suggests, as something of a garrulous buffoon. Yet his introspections are of interest. He is aware that 'there is something going on in me that is independent of me'. This independent entity affects his actions as well as his speech: 'many a time have I willed to do one thing and another has been done';

and he describes himself as 'a blind man pushed from behind'. Other characters in the novel reveal their awareness of this secondary personality, as when one says 'proceed, Azzageddi', and another refers to 'the wild look in his eye'. The talkative philosopher introspects about the relations of his secondary personality to his sleeping life: 'he prowls about in me . . . it is he who talks in my sleep, revealing my secrets'. Clearly he is troubled about his identity, and when asked at what times he feels most himself he replies: 'when I sleep and dream not'. (Unlike Dr Jekyll, Babbalanje accepts his secondary personality with some amiability – an important recognition on Melville's part that not all forms of multiple personality involve a *malevolent* alter ego.)

These are just some examples of the formidable contribution of imaginative literature to our understanding of conflict within the personality. William James referred to such conflict as a process of 'subconscious incubation', in which there is 'a maturing of motives deposited by the experiences of life. When ripe the results hatch out, or burst into flower.' The products of this 'incubation' will be examined next in terms of actual cases of dual or multiple personality. Alongside Pierre Janet, William James and Bernard Hart we now encounter the important work of Morton Prince, who was interested in the wider applications of the concept of dissociation to psychology as a whole.

3
Multiple Personality

She seemed the living counterpart in miniature of Dr Jekyll
and Mr Hyde.

Sir Cyril Burt

The climate of opinion in both science and literature at the turn
of the century invited considerable attention to dissociation
and the multiple personality. *The Brothers Karamazov* and *Deacon
Brodie, or the Double Life* had appeared in 1879. In 1855, the year
of *Markheim*, the French psychologist Ribot had become
interested in multiple personality. *The Strange Case of Dr Jekyll
and Mr Hyde* appeared the following year, and in 1890 William
James's *Principles of Psychology* reported to a wide audience the
case of the Rev. Ansel Bourne. The great French investigator of
hypnosis and hysteria, J. M. Charcot, died in 1893, but in the
same year his distinguished pupil Janet presented his doctoral
dissertation on the mental automatisms of the hysteric. A
strong interest in hypnosis flourished, which certainly pro-
moted the study, and possibly even some of the occurrences, of
dual and multiple personality.

People were intrigued by the resemblances between hypnotically induced automatisms and those which occurred spontaneously. Janet's patient Iréné was a perfect example of how a
sub-system of the personality (born in her case out of a sternly
repressed impulse of rebellion and a yearning for more cheerful
companionship while she nursed her mother) could become
the focus for somnambulisms. Influential Americans were to
learn about such cases when in 1906 Janet lectured at Harvard.
From the adjacent city of Boston emerged the important
studies of Morton Prince. In *The Dissociation of a Personality*
(1906) Prince reported in detail on the most famous case in the
research literature, which he had first described to a fascinated

audience at the 1900 Paris International Congress of Psychology.

The Christine Beauchamp case is packed with psychological interest. There are hallucinations, crystal-gazing imagery, automatic writing and complex amnesias. Christine Beauchamp's three main personalities were B1, B4 and Sally, whom Prince defined respectively as 'the Saint', 'the Woman' and 'the Devil'. B1 was a prim, humourless and guilt-ridden personality. B4 was more human, with recognizable weaknesses including a bad temper. Sally was a mischievous child with a rather perverted sense of humour; as she once remarked of B1, 'she does not enjoy wickedness, I do'. Sally teased, sometimes even tormented, the other sub-systems of Christine.

Morton Prince knew Stevenson's story (his successor as Director of the Harvard Psychological Clinic, Dr Henry Murray, has told me that Prince often spoke of 'Dr J. and Mr H.') and he made considerable use of the concept of co-consciousness in his study of Christine Beauchamp. Sally was more aware of both B1 and B4 than either of them was of her, but she would sometimes make her co-conscious presence felt by intervening with hallucinations or automatic writing. Sally knew all of B1's thoughts but was only able to know about B4's through observation of her actions. During Prince's hypnotic treatment of Christine something most interesting emerged: when hypnotized, both B1 and B4 assumed another personality – but it was the same one (this personality became known as B2).

Introspective knowledge of dreams is denied to most people, but Sally was able to remain awake while B1 and B4 slept. According to Sally, the sleeper would 'imagine then all sorts of things . . . if she remembers them you call them dreams, and the others you don't' (Prince 1906). This testimony is important. Prince himself was loth to make generalizations but half a century later, in 1953, evidence from Azerinsky and Kleitman confirmed his original finding. Because of these later researches we no longer distinguish dreamers from non-dreamers but rather recallers of dreams from non-recallers. Sally had said in 1904: 'I don't see why all the other things she thinks are not just as much dreams as what she remembers.' It is now well established that the majority of human dreaming is, like the majority of human waking thought, lost in forgetfulness. Sally even provided direct introspective reports about the influences of external stimuli: she said that the sleeper 'hears every sound'.

The patient – one of the most famous in the literature of psychology – was a young Radcliffe College student. She was treated by Morton Prince at Boston and her pseudonym 'Beauchamp' was in fact suggested by 'Sally'. Her real name was Clara N. Fowler and she later became Mrs Waterman after marrying a younger assistant of Morton Prince's. Her treatment involved hypnosis, and the case history revealed that at the age of thirteen she had had a fit of nocturnal somnambulism after which she had been brought home in her nightdress by a policeman. A number of sub-systems of her personality emerged during treatment, but we shall concentrate here on B1, B4 and Sally.

There were marked differences of personality between B1 and B4. In most respects they were opposites. B1 was fond of children and old people, while B4 disliked both. They differed in their tastes in food, their choice of clothing, their attitudes to religion and their temperament. B1 was even-tempered, religious and preferred black coffee without sugar. B4 was bad-tempered, irreligious, and drank white coffee with sugar. Both had to contend with Sally, and Sally usually won. Sometimes Sally would assume possession, but at other times she would merely maintain her co-conscious existence. She is described by Prince as 'a child of nature, childlike in every way'. Unlike the rather fragile Miss Beauchamp herself in her B1 personality, Sally was a healthy young girl, cheerful and never fatigued., She 'enjoyed life hugely'. She might take control for minutes, or for hours at a time, and she had a deep contempt for B1. The B1 and B4 personalities experienced discontinuities in the passage of time. After these amnesic periods, events would seem to occur without cause. Sally, who was either on stage or co-consciously present, took positive pleasure in creating embarrassing situations and then withdrawing.

Sally could inflict imagery on the other personalities in the form of hallucinations. Her interventions with automatic writing are reminiscent of the similar intrusions by Mr Hyde on Dr Jekyll. The content of an 'ultimatum' which B4 sent to Sally one summer is revealing: it demanded no more interference with letters through the post, no more hallucinations and 'no more snakes or spiders'. (On one occasion knowing Miss Beauchamp's horror of spiders, Sally had collected some, put them into a box and posted them to her. Six spiders emerged from the parcel.) The B4 ultimatum also insisted that Sally confine herself to her weekly allowance, and allow B4 to choose her own food, clothing and friends. For her part, the quick-tempered B4 found Sally's own friends 'very objectionable'.

Sally's automatic writing intrusions seriously impeded the efforts of the other personalities to communicate with Dr Prince. As B1 wrote on one occasion: 'Pardon, I can't rewrite. Sally has spoiled this.' In another letter, well might B4 write, '. . . in haste'! Sally's contemptuous dislike for the other personalities was manifested in a variety of other ways. On one occasion she took a car six miles out into the country, abandoned it, and then 'woke up' her other personalities. They had a long and exhausting walk, since Sally had ensured that there was no money in their pocket for the fare home. After B1 had sat up late at night knitting, Sally would emerge and sit up still later unpicking the knitting. This could go on for several nights.

Morton Prince recorded that 'the war clouds were gathering thick and fast . . . letters of complaint poured in on me.' Nevertheless Sally had moments of altruism. On one occasion she intervened to save B1 from suicide. In her despair B1 had gone to bed with the gas jet full on; Sally arrived, jumped from the bed, opened the window, turned off the gas and saved the lives of both of them. However, Prince's therapy was aimed at the integration of Miss Beauchamp's personality, and this had to be through the 'death' of Sally. Sally kept a diary, and she described herself as being 'squeezed'. Prince recorded this with some regret: he seemed to have developed an affection for Sally, as for an attractive if delinquent child.

Discontinuities in the sense of passage of time are prominent. When B4 first emerged she did not know either Morton Prince or the surroundings of his consulting room. Prince likened her to Rip Van Winkle, who had no idea that time had passed while he was asleep. Sally 'was invaluable as an informer' about events in these periodic amnesic episodes; she had a continuous memory from early infancy, including memory of the six years for which the B4 personality had amnesia.

The relation of 'possession' by evil spirits to dissociation will be discussed in the next chapter. There were occasions when Miss Beauchamp exhibited at least a measure of half belief in this possibility, as when she sadly said to Morton Prince, 'like those poor people of old I must be possessed of devils' (Prince 1906). In the personality of B4 she had a particularly alarming experience of this kind. She was sitting looking at herself in a mirror when she noticed a smile on her face that was 'diabolical and uncanny'. She realized that it was not herself, and began to talk to 'it'. This proved ineffective, so with the aid of a pencil in her hand she began a strange conversation. She spoke in the personality of B4; replies came via the pencil in the form of automatic writing. The person in the mirror, or at least the system that controlled the replies, was Sally.

Records of the case include some of Miss Beauchamp's more mundane tribulations. Dressing, for example, might take up to two hours. It was not merely a question of choosing clothes acceptable to whichever personality happened to be on the stage at the time; they often had to be found where 'somebody' else had left or hidden them. Bathing could take a long time, too, since B1 did not accept that she had had a bath unless she had herself consciously been present. Meals involved similar

44

troubles, given the marked differences in food preference of B1 and B4, plus the tiresome interventions of Sally.

The basis of this dissociation Morton Prince found in mental conflict: 'beginning with a rebellious group of wishes and ideas . . . another self comes into existence' (1901). Sally regarded B1 as a weakling and a sentimentalist, and she developed strong hatred for B4, upon whom she frequently poured abuse. Prince reported finding pieces of paper covered with scribbled messages between the two of them. Conflicts between the personalities were also apparent in Miss Beauchamp's crystal-gazing visions. These visions would relate to past events, and this caused trouble. On one occasion B1 had a crystal vision of 'herself' smoking a cigarette – an actual event involving Sally, for which B1 had amnesia – and she responded to this with considerable horror.

One can sympathize with Morton Prince's indulgent affection for the Sally personality: she was capable of considerable malice, but on the whole she was not a 'Mrs Hyde'. There is far less appeal in the secondary personality of May Naylor, whose case was reported by Sir Cyril Burt in *The Young Delinquent* in 1937. The events relate to one morning in 1917 when 'Mr Naylor', a highly respectable foreman, was greeted on arrival at work by two furious colleagues. The first demanded: 'Look here, Naylor, how long have you been carrying on with my wife?' The second produced some filthy sheets of paper multiplying the accusation in equally filthy language. Mr Naylor was protesting to the two indignant men that he didn't even know that they were married, when a third victim arrived. The letters all ended with the signature 'May Naylor'. Mr Naylor himself had been receiving a series of abusive letters, all signed with the name of his only daughter. Other accusations had been sent in writing both to his employer and to the vicar of his church.

Burt, who was then psychologist to the London County Council, was called in to investigate the girl at her school. He found a happy, inoffensive little child of nine. May Naylor was a model pupil who attended school with punctuality, and a careful speller who wrote in a neat hand which was in every respect quite different from the ugly scrawls received by her father and others. Her score on tests showed superior intellectual ability, and she had well-above-average scores on attainment tests for reading, spelling and comprehension. She did, however, have strong visual imagery. When she told Burt that her favourite flower was lily of the valley 'so white, and pure, and clean', he became suspicious. During hypnosis she reproduced the content of one unopened letter, word for word. Later she tearfully repudiated it. After this the letters continued to appear but under the signature of 'May Lomax' (the maiden name of May's mother). Burt set to in an attempt to integrate the personalities of the two Mays. The one was pure and fastidiously correct, the other coarse, revengeful and foul-mouthed: 'she seemed the living counterpart, in miniature, of Dr Jekyll and Mr Hyde' (Burt 1937). The case responded to successful treatment, and the letters ceased.

From the malice of May Naylor it is something of a relief to turn to the better-known case of Eve White. Her secondary personality, Eve Black, is discussed by the investigators Thigpen and Cleckley, whose first account of the case appeared in an article of 1954. Mrs White came to them as a colourless young woman of about twenty-five. Her presenting symptoms were headaches and hallucination, for which Eve Black later assumed full responsibility. Miss Eve Black, who always retained her maiden name, emerged as a Sally-like personality, vivacious, irresponsible, unreliable and likeable; she was co-consciously aware of Eve White. The therapists' first major problem was how to tell Eve White that she shared her body with a totally different person – and furthermore, someone whose repertoire of sentiments embraced contempt for Mr White, the husband, and a hearty dislike for Mrs White's little daughter Bonny.

Eve Black took great pleasure in producing amnesic periods for Eve White, as a result of which Mrs White would receive huge bills for expensive clothes she would never have dreamed of buying. Eve Black's intervention was less wayward on one occasion when she managed to save Eve White from killing them both. Eve White was trying to cut her veins with a razor; Eve Black struggled to 'get out' and succeeded in knocking the razor to the floor. She remarked afterwards to her therapist: 'I think she meant business, Doc.' On the whole, like Sally in the Beauchamp case, Eve Black emerges as a somewhat younger personality than the dominant one, and there is evidence of the same kindly, perhaps indulgent, affection towards her from the therapists.

The integration of Eve was achieved for a while through the emergence of a more mature and more emotionally robust third personality, Jane. Jane was succeeded by Evelyn, after which there was both a divorce and a new marriage. Events up until this time were recorded by the Evelyn personality under the name 'Evelyn Lancaster'. The dissociations of Eve continued. Over twenty years or so there were allegedly as many as twenty-two different identities. There were differences in age, and also in certain bodily phenomena such as the presence of freckles or allergies. In one of her identities Eve was blind; in several others she exhibited artistic talents, and she painted in a variety of styles. After more than twenty years of anonymity Eve identified herself to the *Washington Post*.

One of the most interesting cases of multiple personality is that of Sybil Dorsett, who was successfully treated by a New York psychoanalyst, Dr Cornelia Wilbur. In Sybil's case there were allegedly sixteen different personalities, some of whom differed in body-image as well as behaviour. Two of them, Mike and Sid, were boys; there was an infantile personality, Ruthie; Vanessa was a tall red-head. As in other cases we encounter intrapsychic conflict, time-discontinuity problems, amnesia and hallucination. Sybil herself was described as 'a depleted person'; she had had an appalling childhood with a cruel, psychotic mother (one of her sub-personalities, Peggy Lou, emerged as self-assertive and often angry). The personality of Victoria, or Vicky, in this case is particularly interesting. She resembles the mature Jane of the Eve case, and co-operated closely with the therapist. Vicky 'knew everything': that is, she was co-consciously present while the other personalities held the stage. On arriving for therapy she would make such comments as 'I don't need therapy: the others are neurotic, but I'm not. But I do want to help'. Of the depleted Sybil she remarked, 'I have to stand up for her.'

The Sybil case presented the usual problems with money matters, choice of friends, time discontinuities and conflict of interests. (Once when Sybil was trying to cross the road – one personality wanting to cross and another not wanting to – a baffled traffic officer called out crossly, 'For goodness sake, lady, make up your mind.' He was hardly to know that what he was dealing with was two very real different people, not just one.) Sybil was enabled to 'meet' her various other selves through listening to recordings of their voices. Along with psychoanalytic free-association methods, Dr Wilbur used chemical abreaction (see Chapter 10) and hypnotism to help penetrate the amnesic barriers. Since the different personalities varied in age the therapy also had to involve among other things a process of 'growing up' for the baby Ruthie if the personalities were to be integrated satisfactorily. The full story of Sybil's life and of Dr Wilbur's treatment of her was subsequently written up by a scientific journalist in book form (Schreiber 1975) and makes fascinating reading.

In a case of this kind we have to face the problem of suggestion. Quite obviously the interests and presuppositions of the therapist or investigator can reinforce certain developments, even precipitate the emergence of additional sub-systems. On the other hand I suspect that there are many instances where people who could and perhaps should be considered in multiple-personality terms are diagnosed otherwise. In the three cases of Christine, Eve and Sybil we find many common features. Each of the initial personalities seems to have been a depressed, depleted individual, with many problems and a strong motivation to escape to a new identity. Time discontinuities played a major part in all three cases, and in each there occurred hallucinations stemming from the imagery and thought-processes of various sub-systems. All women, they were lucky to be born into a society that would not instantly condemn them as witches or 'possessed'.

Multiple personality remains a rarity. As a concept in psychological diagnosis it must be handled with care. As we have seen the psychoanalytic movement has never been impressed either with the concept of dissociation or with hypnotic methods of treatment. But it is my belief that such cases as we have discussed have helped to provide scientists and therapists with a new category into which some people may *need* to fall. With multiple personality back on the map, some commoner forms of dissociative behaviour – such as automatic writing, crystal-gazing imagery, fugues, nocturnal somnambulisms and those states of 'possession' that are still widely reported – may be seen in a new light. I shall try to show later how well the dissociation model fits some of Freud's own early cases, but at this point it may be appropriate and useful to pause and classify some of the phenomena we have been considering. It will be apparent by now that not all multiple-personality cases exhibit the classic Jekyll/Hyde syndrome. A typology involving five differing kinds of multiple personality may be attempted.

The Alter Ego
Here we must remember the influence of labels, and in particular the temptation for people at certain times and in certain societies to attribute demonological inspiration to anyone whose beliefs or behaviour differ markedly from their own. The legend of the 'damnable life and deserved death' of Faust, the scholar-magician of the sixteenth century who sold his soul to the devil, has a long history. Faust caught the imagination of both Marlowe and Goethe, and would certainly have been part of the heritage of Dostoevsky and Stevenson. His story may

well have contributed, if only subconsciously, to the hallucinatory devils of Dr Jekyll and Ivan Karamazov.

The demonological tradition has a significant bearing on scientific study of multiple personality. Abnormal behaviour, like heretical or unorthodox beliefs, has to be explained somehow. As we have seen, and as Morton Prince himself was quick to point out, had she lived at a different time Miss Beauchamp would almost certainly have been thought possessed – and might have believed that herself. Her Sally personality was most of the time no more than a troublesome child, but she had a darker side which might – in an appropriately superstitious environment – have been interpreted in terms of poltergeist phenomena. During the spring of 1901, for example, the B4 personality made vigorous attempts to suppress Sally, and Sally fought back. Sally would make the nights hideous for B4, throwing the bedding on the floor or heaping piles of furniture on the bed, and then changing herself back to B4. She would attack during the day too, inflicting gloomy or terrifying hallucinations on B4, who saw in the street 'endless processions of black robed figures'. Similarly, B4 might lose the use of her right hand, and be forced to do everything left-handedly. On one occasion B4 showed her arms to Dr Prince: there were 'numerous and ugly scratches extending the whole length' of them, made by some sharp instrument. In these phenomena we find some evidence of an aversion between the personalities involving intense malice and hatred: a supernatural interpretation in terms of demon possession or poltergeists would be quite understandable. The Ivan Karamazov dissociation, through Dostoevksy's insights, provides an excellent model for the understanding of this type of dual personality. Thus on one occasion Ivan declares to his brother Alyosha that if the devil does not exist, but man has created him, then man has created him in his own image and likeness. Later Ivan tells his brother 'He is myself, Alyosha, all that's base in me, all that is mean and contemptible'.

The Regressive Type

In some instances the subsidiary personalities seem to spring from earlier developmental stages in the life of the patient. An extreme case is represented in the instance of 'Mrs X', cited by Taylor and Martin (1944) in their survey. One of the personalities was a one-year-old infant: the original investigator photographed his patient – a mature woman – in this personality, learning to walk! Features of the Mary Reynolds case, and others, indicate this type of developmentally regressive sub-personality. The attitudes of investigators like Morton Prince to 'Sally' and Thigpen and Cleckley to 'Eve Black' strongly resemble those of an over-indulgent parent. They appear to have experienced genuine distress in having to destroy the colourful child even in order to create an integrated mature adult.

The baby 'Ruthie' in the Sybil dissociations is a clear instance of a regressive sub-personality: in the course of hypnotic therapy designed to integrate Sybil, it was necessary for the therapist to manipulate the sense of time to make Ruthie 'grow up'. Throughout this case it is apparent that the mature and helpful 'Vicky' personality adopted a motherly attitude to the baby Ruthie. In one of the few places where Freud discusses multiple personality he suggests an explanation in terms of the different developmental stages of the individual assuming autonomous control of the personality, in succession to one another. This formulation admirably fits the 'regressive type'.

The Boy Within

Carl Jung views the personality as a state of equilibrium between conscious and unconscious. In his view, woman (consciously feminine) has within her an unconscious masculine aspect, the animus; man (consciously masculine) has an unconscious feminine aspect, the anima. A rather striking example of an animus sub-personality occurred in the case of Hélène Smith, to be discussed more fully later. Hélène as a child had been rescued from a fierce dog by a man around whom she then developed wish-fulfilling fantasies. The man's personality, in the form of 'Leopold', recurred as an adviser and protector; in the dissociation it would take over and assume control when Hélène herself was in some way threatened. In the Sybil case we have the two male personalities, Mike and Sid, who showed considerable resentment at their suppression in the course of the therapy designed to integrate the female body. Subsidiary personalities of the opposite sex are rare: in their survey Taylor and Martin found only nine instances in the sixty-four cases they discuss.

The Imaginary Companion

The outstanding case of this kind is that of Sybil, whose miserable home life and experience of maternal cruelty were enough to encourage several imaginary companions. These included the assertive and often angry Peggy Lou; Vicky, who was much better able to look after herself than the depleted personality Sybil; and the rather charming pair, Marcia and Vanessa. On one occasion the therapist complimented Marcia and Vanessa on their sense of humour. Vanessa declared roundly that you *had* to have a sense of humour to survive in Sybil's family, in that 'God-fearing and man hating' town with its false and sickly sentiment: 'there was so much sugar that I suffered from diabetes of the soul'. The relations of the sixteen sub-personalities of Sybil were, on the whole, extremely good. They seem to represent highly atypical manifestations of the imaginary companion phenomenon.

Romantic Fantasy

This type overlaps with the preceding one and also, in cases like Leopold, with the regressive type. Hunter (1964) has discussed how an individual may build up a role for himself, and then step into it: he makes for himself a new identity, which in many of the classic cases is an escape from some sort of deprivation, frustration or emotional bleakness. Perhaps this was the case with Ansel Bourne. Certainly it seems to have been so with 'Spanish Maria': Maria had been fascinated by Spain, particularly by a young man of Spanish parentage around whom she built up a fantasy; a secondary personality eventually emerged, which she believed to be the reincarnation of a Spanish gypsy dancer who had led an exciting and adventurous life.

Earlier we discussed type-3 dissociation – the fugue – as a form of flight from one personality and its problems to another way of life. Phenomena of this general type sometimes involve the police and the law. During the mid 1970s there was considerable public interest in the case of Mr John Stonehouse, British member of Parliament and former cabinet minister. He disappeared from Miami Beach, Florida, and was subsequently arrested in Australia. He was extradited from Australia and tried at the Old Bailey on various charges. The defence in both instances claimed dissociation of the personality. In his autobiography (1976), Mr Stonehouse reports that in Miami he 'broke away from the Stonehouse burdens . . . I was reborn a simple, uncluttered Joe Markham'. As Markham, Stonehouse travelled to Australia, then to Copenhagen, then back to Melbourne via Moscow and Singapore. Then a third personality, 'Clive Mildoon', took over. The motivation described in the book is that of the fugue: 'I felt England had become oppressive . . . we develop cloaks as we go along, we put on clothes, we put on new personalities, we develop attitudes as a result of the jobs we do.'

At the Old Bailey trial various expert witnesses testified. Amongst them was Dr Lionel Haward, a leading British forensic psychologist. In his testimony he explained how it is possible for parts of the nervous system to be cut off, and how this can result in a change of identity. He referred to the Eve case as an instance. Another witness, the psychiatrist Dr R. D. Laing, discussed 'splitting of the personality into two or multiple pieces', and is reported to have said that the mind becomes 'compartmentalized so that in one compartment the pain is not felt' (Stonehouse 1976). Stonehouse's secretary testified that he spoke of himself in the third person, always 'he' or 'him' and never 'I'. He had explained to her that he had 'become' Mr Markham. Mr Stonehouse himself records the pleasure Markham felt in such actions as queuing up for his vaccination certificate or booking in at an hotel, which established his identity: 'Markham really existed.' Full details of this case are not yet available. While we await them I would suggest that the recorded facts are wholly compatible with a type-2 or type-3 automatism. Other forms of dissociation may also involve the law. One young offender, a girl of eighteen, told me in interview how ever since early childhood two different people had existed within her. One was 'a dear little self', the other 'really bad'. The 'bad self' first revealed itself by 'talking back' to the teacher in school. Later its hostility to school and teachers resulted in more delinquent behaviour, including setting fire to a classroom and causing damages estimated at $12,000. A second arson offence, again involving a classroom, followed soon afterwards. On occasions she inflicted a considerable amount of malicious damage; several incidents involved throwing stones through a great number of windows. She also devoted much time to slashing the tyres of motor vehicles, and her preference was for police cars. This was particularly odd in that her other self had a strong ambition at the time to be a policewoman. She was also given to shoplifting. She explained in interview that she 'didn't really have power to stop', and that she 'used to get scared when it came on'; when the 'good part' of her took over she would 'regret it'. Of interest in the case of this young woman – who had by now a formidable history of impulsive crime – was her interest in imaginative writing. She explained how, when she wrote, 'the pen itself did most of the work'.

More extreme is the case of an offender – in this instance a patient in a security psychiatric hospital – who had committed murder. He told me in one interview that he had no memory of having killed his victim at all, nor any awareness of the many stab wounds he had in fact inflicted. His response to my question whether, if released, he might do it again, was chilling. He replied, with every sign of full sincerity: 'I don't really know.' All he could say was, 'I really do hope I wouldn't.' The crime in question was motiveless by ordinary standards: the murderer himself seemed quite unable to throw any light upon it (McKellar 1968). This case bears an uncanny resemblance to the quite terrifying portrait of an 'innocent' child-murderer in Fritz Lang's classic film *'M'*. In neither case can we be certain that multiple personality was the cause, but the evidence does seem to point in that direction.

Cases of multiple personality, however rare, continue to be reported. One such case may be taken to illustrate a new approach to this phenomenon. The investigators in question (Larmore, Ludwig and Cain 1977) estimate that there had been about two hundred reported instances of multiple personality by the time of their own publication. Their newer techniques are of interest, in the historical context of such cases. Morton Prince, in studying Miss Beauchamp, was severely limited by the methods available. Thigpen and Cleckley, working with the Eve case, were more fortunate. They measured the intelligence of the initial three main personalities; they assessed the semantic differential in the concepts and styles of thinking of Eve White, Eve Black and Jane; they used film and sound-recording to 'introduce' the three personalities to one another. For their part the investigators of the 'Faith' case (discussed below) used personality testing. In addition they made a study of the physiological differences in the woman's body when one or other of the personalities was in control.

The primary personality of Faith, a thirty-five-year-old Kentucky woman, was admitted to hospital with very many medical problems. She had a recurrent history of attempts to harm herself, and had made no fewer than seven suicide efforts. When interviewed she reported an awareness of 'someone within trying to get control'. She suffered from time discontinuities with amnesic gaps ranging from several minutes to periods of weeks. The secondary personality which emerged was of the malevolent alter ego kind. This was 'Alicia' who believed herself to be an agent of Satan, sent to take over the body and soul of Faith. Alicia would assume control especially during periods of alcoholic intoxication. She had been responsible for attempts made to stab both Faith's husband and her five-year-old child. No warning had been given for these autonomous impulses. During the previous five years, a third sub-system had emerged as 'Alicia-Faith', a system dominated by Alicia and described by the investigators as 'a fearful little girl' (her fearfulness was confirmed by physiological measurements). There was also a colourful fourth personality called the 'Guardian Angel'. This claimed to be the protector of Faith; it had strong religious sentiments, and claimed to have the power to communicate directly with God; it was co-conscious, had full awareness of the other three personalities, and also claimed the power to foresee the future. The tests, both psychological and physiological, satisfied the investigators of the inadequacy of any explanation in terms of deception or mere role playing. One standard test used, the MMPI, revealed that all four personalities had bizarre features of the psychotic kind.

Belief systems, including the diagnostic preferences of the investigators themselves, are obviously important here. This particular case would seem to some people to lie intermediate between hysterical neurosis and schizophrenic psychosis – classifications which will be considered in a later chapter. Also relevant are occult belief systems, and the supernatural characteristics claimed by the sub-systems. There are the belief systems of the investigators, those of the patient herself and those of the community to consider. Faith's own background appears to have been of a fundamentalist and religiously naïve kind. For their part, her investigators treated their patient within the context of naturalistic psychiatry and physiology. Alternative interpretations will always be made.

'Possession' and 'multiple personality' may have a great deal in common, and as we shall see in the next chapter the demonological approach by no means died out with the passing of the Middle Ages.

4
Demonology,
Possession and Exorcism

Multiple personality is no new thing. It is as old as demonic
possession, lycanthropy, the frenzy of the oracle, the superstitious reverence for epileptics.

J. Laird

In ancient Persia, Zoroaster (Zarathustra) taught of an eternal
war between good and evil. The forces of light were personified
in Ormuzd, and those of darkness in Ahriman with his attendant demons. Zoroastrian tradition developed an elaborate
system of evil spirits, and also a form of exorcism. Holy water
was used on one part of the body after another: the possessing
demon would be driven by it from the right shoulder to the left,
from there to the armpit, thence to the chest, and ultimately
out of the body from its last stronghold, the toe. In his *History of
Magic* (1948) Seligman testifies to the survival of Zoroastrian
rituals into Christian times. He gives as one illustration a
seventeenth-century exorcism at the court of the King of
France. The demon concerned (in this case Beelzebub)
escaped from the possessed woman's mouth under exorcism in
the shape of a fly.

The notion of a malevolent deity with attendant evil spirits is
one of man's most ancient and most resilient archetypes, and
traditions of possession and exorcism are deeply embedded in
all the most influential religions. Ancient Egypt had its evil
deity, Set, who brought about the destruction of Osiris.
Buddhist tradition tells how Gautama Buddha was tempted by
Mara. In Christianity we learn of the temptation of Jesus by
Satan, and how men possessed of the devil were exorcised. We
read in *The Koran* how Satan's Islamic counterpart, Iblis, was

likewise a fallen angel, a conspirator against Allah. In a symposium on trance and possession states published in 1968, the Islamic scholar Eickelman records that Islam has 'always affirmed' the ability of supernatural agents, including demons, to possess human beings. This same symposium includes parallel contributions from Christian theology. Both the Roman Catholic and the Protestant contributors concerned adopt a positive attitude towards the concept of demonic possession. The causes of this demonological standpoint are too complex to be given exhaustive treatment here; but so far as the notion of 'possession' is involved some attention must be paid to it.

An alternative tradition is that of naturalistic science, which grew out of the inquiries of the Greek philosophers, in particular Aristotle (385–322 BC). Aristotle taught, as regards psychology and ethics, that the raw materials of human nature are ethically neutral. Virtues, including the four Greek virtues of temperance, courage, justice and wisdom, are learned habits. And so are the vices. The values of Ancient Greece, its logic, its sciences and its philosophy were communicated by Aristotle to his pupils. One such pupil was the young Alexander who, long before the heyday of Imperial Rome, established a great empire extending from Greece and Italy to Northern India, the foothills of the Caucasus and Egypt. Alexander's armies overcame the powerful Persians, and Greek culture flourished for a time. Nevertheless Zoroastrian and other forms of demonology persisted. Later, when Christianity spread, it discouraged alternative religions with demonological fervour. Early Christian fathers of the Church were against Christians entering, or even going near, pagan temples, since this might expose them to the evil spirits that haunted them. At times Christianity, like other great religions, has done much to relieve men and women of their fears of demonic possession; but this has not always been so. For example Augustine, Bishop of Hippo (AD 345–430), who despite his conversion to Christianity was still under the influence of Persian ideas, did much to impose demonology on the simple believer. This early

Christian tendency to identify rival gods with evil spirits is brought vividly to life in Milton's *Paradise Lost*. The pagan gods appear as the fellow conspirators of Satan, banished with him and now his attendant demons in the infernal regions of fire over which he rules. From the standpoint of naturalistic science within psychology, we have seen how Jung conceived of 'the shadow' or malevolent alter ego – the aspect of himself man most wishes to repudiate. Perhaps, as Dostoevksy's Ivan Karamazov argued with such eloquence, man creates his own evil deity, personified in his own image.

Demonology, with its ideas of possession and exorcism, is still very much alive. The anthropologist Erika Bourguignon (1973) has charted the geographical positions of cults and religions that accept spirit possession: her maps cover parts of Africa, Afro-America and the Caribbean, India, Asia and both South and North America. Jung visited Africa, and he too has some interesting comments to make. He was impressed with the gaiety and general cheerfulness he encountered in the various African peoples. There in the sunshine, they told him, they enjoyed their lives. But this joy and cheerfulness seemed to depart at sunset. In the darkness they were beset by fears of the evil spirits of the night. When sunrise returned, both light and cheerful living began again. As he travelled northwards, Jung tells us, he began to speculate on this association of evil with darkness and good with light. For the first time he felt that he had begun to understand sun worship, or at least the part played by the sun as a symbol of something that pushed back the forces of darkness. Elsewhere he expresses the idea that primitive man's mind, together with his fears, is not in his head but outside it, projected out there into the jungle. I suspect that there may be an aspect of that 'primitive mind' in all of us: when we are alone, the pressure of darkness does much to stimulate imagination and fearful imagery.

Of interest here is a fascinating autobiography by Dawa Norbu (1974) in which he tells of his childhood in rural Tibet. He writes that 'the Tibetans believe that evil spirits can enter the bodies of human beings', and remembers watching a tantric lama driving an evil spirit from the body of Namgyal, his family's next-door neighbour. The demon resisted exorcism for a time, by refusing to give his name. I myself had an interesting conversation with a patient in the State of New Mexico. This man, a Navajo Indian, had been treated in the usual way within his reservation, by an operation 'to remove the evil spirits'. He was now receiving modern psychiatric treatment, which fitted in rather better with his own beliefs.

Belief systems are all important in considering relationships between dissociation and possession. A case from India reported in 1956 by Alexander may be taken as an illustration. Dr Alexander himself interpreted it as an instance of multiple personality, while the Asian girl, Soosan, and her relatives interpreted it in terms of spirit possession. Yet we do not need to go as far as Norbu's rural Tibet or Soosan's rural India to find such interpretations. The psychiatrist Sargant (1973) reports the case of a woman alive in London today who believes herself possessed of the spirits of famous composers. Mozart, Beethoven and others dictate music to her. While her beliefs are obviously not shared by Dr Sargant, a small sub-culture of firm believers appears to be most effective in reinforcing an occult interpretation.

Some people still choose to interpret co-consciousness, multiple personality and other dissociative phenomena in terms of possession by some disembodied entity, or spirit control. One of the most interesting cases of this kind was the spiritual medium Daniel Dunglas Home (1833–1886). Home does not seem to have deserved Robert Browning's poem about him entitled 'Mr Sludge the Medium': he did not take money for his séances, and there are no records of his ever being 'exposed'. The odd happenings within his mental life seem greatly to have disturbed his aunt, with whom he lived. She approached no fewer than three ministers of different denominations; none succeeded in his exorcism, and she ejected him from her home. Much has been written about Home testifying to his powers of clairvoyance, and to his capacity to reproduce, for example, the autograph of Napoleon I. He seems to have been well respected by many European rulers including the Tsar, the King of Prussia and Napoleon III. It is difficult to dismiss a man like Home in terms of simple fraud or stage magic. Moreover Home showed something rather rare in this field, a cautious and critical attitude of his own towards 'psychic phenomena'. Like others possessed of a highly unusual personality, and strangely autonomous features in their mental life, he does not seem to have wholly enjoyed these attributes. They were beyond his control.

Among others who would reject the idea of 'dissociation' in favour of 'possession' may be mentioned Dion Fortune (the late Mrs V. M. Penry-Evans). In her book *Psychic Self-Defence* (1930) Dion Fortune discusses the effective counter-measures that can be taken against 'psychic attack'. Such attack, she argues, may take place under four main conditions: if one is in a place where 'psychic' forces are concentrated, as in some 'hauntings'; if one deals with people handling such forces; if one 'goes out to meet the unknown'; or if one falls victim to certain pathological conditions. This last case she illustrates by citing people who interpret their own or other people's epilepsy as a struggle with some entity of the astral world. She herself relates an incident in which she got involved with a 'simulacrum' or thought form, a cat-like materialization which fortunately disappeared after an exorcism. Many of us who would wish to retain a rather more cautious attitude than hers to such phenomena as vampires, werewolves, poltergeists and projections of the astral body during sleep may nevertheless agree with Dion Fortune that the average person is out of his depth in these matters. She distinguishes three phases of reaction to the 'psychic'. First there is the belief that all is superstition and fraud. Then, when scepticism has been undermined, one is prepared to believe anything. Finally, there may emerge an attitude of good judgment and discrimination. It has to be said that not everyone moves on from the second phase.

W. P. Blatty's book *The Exorcist* was published in 1972, and the widely screened film of the book had a dramatic effect on impressionable audiences. In the book, an anxious mother approaches a priest of the Church of Rome, believing her daughter to be 'possessed'. She asks about exorcism. The priest, Father Karras, is exceedingly sceptical. He suggests that the first thing she needs is a time machine to take her back to the sixteenth century, as 'it doesn't happen any more'. Father Karras insists on elaborate medical tests; but he is finally convinced, and manages to persuade an even more sceptical bishop to permit an exorcism, provided that it follow strict Catholic procedures. Many years earlier the Bishop of Exeter – aware that such procedures had not been established in the Church of England – had set up a commission. The Exeter Report of 1958 suggested guidelines for Anglican priests in matters involving exorcism. The published report was edited by Dom Robert Petitpierre, a Dominican expert on exorcism. The Commission recommended a number of safeguards including insistence on close medical collaboration, permission from the bishop of the area, and the use of trained and experienced exorcists only. The vital importance of expert knowledge and strict standards in this matter was given tragic emphasis in 1974, during an epidemic of seemingly uncontrolled exorcisms in England.

In one small town in Yorkshire a group of people who called themselves the 'Christian Fellowship' became involved in demonic exorcisms conducted by a twenty-two-year-old girl. She believed herself possessed of the holy spirit and began 'speaking in tongues' (glossolalia). The group convinced itself that one of its members, a man I shall call 'A.B.', was demonically possessed and needed exorcism. Not for nothing do the Church of Rome, the Exeter Commission of the Church of England and expert occultists like Dion Fortune advise caution in these matters. The exorcism failed. A.B. was then submitted to an 'official' exorcism, on the decision of two local clergymen and their helpers; it was conducted in the vestry of an Anglican church. After this attempted exorcism A.B. returned home, to murder his wife and the only other living thing in the house, a dog. The children had fortunately been removed earlier that night. At the trial for murder which followed, the prosecuting barrister referred to the night of exorcism as 'like a throwback to the Middle Ages'. The defence described the exorcist team as 'a group of terrified souls who simply fed neurosis to a neurotic'. A psychiatrist expert witness testified that 'if he had not been exposed to this, and had been treated medically, he would not have killed' (*Yorkshire Post*, 26 March 1975).

The accused A.B. was committed to Broadmoor Special (Security) Hospital. Afterwards the Coroner took the unusual step of reopening the inquest in the form of a public inquiry. As I was in Yorkshire at the time I was able to attend, as a member of the general public. From the legal, psychological and demonological standpoints the inquiry was an exceptionally interesting event. The Coroner conducted proceedings with firm dignity, legal Counsel represented various parties concerned and testimony was taken on oath. The man A.B. had clearly believed himself demoniacally possessed. This belief appears to have been shared by the Anglican and Methodist clergymen who had conducted the official exorcism. At one stage during the exorcism proceedings the Methodist had recommended obtaining psychiatric help, but his suggestion was not taken up.

One of the exorcist team claimed that as many as forty to fifty demons had been 'cast out' of the man. Three demons had resisted: 'insanity', 'murder' and 'violence'. In considering whether or not to conduct the exorcism the group had decided to apply the age-old test, and they had exorcised because the devil named himself. At the extended inquest Counsel for the police brought out through skilful cross-examination of one witness the fact that A.B. was lying in the vestry in the position of a cross, with people praying over him. The window was left open 'for the spirits to go out'. One of the exorcists declared under cross-examination her belief that 'Satan himself was speaking' through A.B. Another was questioned about what he now thought of events:

Answer: The result of demon possession.
Coroner: Even now?
Answer: Even now.

At the extended inquest Dom Robert Petitpierre appeared as an expert witness. Questioned about the Bishop of Exeter's report he told how at one point as many as 3,000 copies had sold in a fortnight. Counsel emphasized how easy the report had been to come by, with its rules and guidelines. Dom Robert was asked about the 'forty to fifty demons'. His own opinion was more cautious: 'I would say just a couple of demons stirring things up . . . I've heard that language used in connection with genuine cases.' He strongly supported the need on such occasions for medical collaboration, and also for after-care. In his summing up the Coroner stressed that it had been 'a tragedy that psychiatric help was not sought'. The exorcism itself was 'well-intentioned, but tragic'. His conclusion was most emphatic: 'The message is clear. This must *never* be allowed to happen again . . . This case draws attention to the dangers inherent in certain highly charged and emotional forms of religious ecstasy . . .' He spoke of 'special problems in others' which were 'not for well-intentioned amateurs to meddle with'. At the time, A.B. had had 'no criminal or evil intent towards his wife. In the circumstances the proper verdict is one of death by misadventure' (*Daily Telegraph*, 24 April 1975).

It seems a matter for serious regret that even today there are so few safeguards. The exorcism of *places* believed to be 'haunted' – if it makes people feel happier – may be therapeutically helpful. Exorcism of *people* who are believed to be 'possessed' is a far more dangerous exercise, above all in the hands of amateurs, however well-intentioned. Since the Church of England was involved in the case described it may be noted that a Canon of the Church of 1603 forbids exorcisms, except by leave of the local bishop. The Church of Rome has always required such permission. Even those prepared to accept demonological belief systems advise extreme caution, as did the expert witness at the extended inquest – and as indeed did the fictional Father Karras in Blatty's novel. Dion Fortune has said that 'psychic attacks are comparatively rare things': we must not assume them 'until we have excluded all the other things it can possibly be'.

From European believers in demons and exorcisms, let us return for a moment to those other parts of the world we have mentioned. In 1972 Bourguignon conducted a cross-cultural study of some 400 non-Western societies. She found evidence of 'some institutionalized form of dissociation' in no less than 89 per cent of them! Other investigators give substantial support to this overall finding. In the same year Leon, for example, found a widespread belief in Latin America that physical as well as psychiatric illnesses are due to possession by evil spirits. He noted the vigour of the Pentecostal movement (with 'speaking in tongues' as a central feature) in such places as Mexico and Brazil.

We have already noted that the 'possession trance' is in many parts of Africa an accepted phenomenon. The person in trance is believed to be inhabited by the spirit of some supernatural being which is looked to for guidance as were the oracles of ancient Greece. After this period in an altered mental state the person returns to his or her normal identity, usually with amnesia for the experience. Detailed studies of the possession trances of some African societies have been conducted by the anthropologist Leonora Greenbaum. She compared societies which exhibited the possession-trance phenomenon with those which did not, and related both to a variety of factors including the incidence of slavery. The phenomenon appeared most often in the context of an extremely rigid social structure which exerted strict control over the activities of its members; guidance through possessing spirits fitted well into such a framework – it relieved the individual of personal responsibility for his decisions, and helped to solve problems without disturbing the established social order.

These supernatural guiding spirits of the possession trance bring us on from the demons of 'mediaeval' superstition to a rather different interpretation of dissociative behaviour. As we shall see in the next chapter, the theory of reincarnation provides *an* answer to quite a number of curious phenomena – and it is sanctioned by some of the oldest religions in the world.

5
Theories of Reincarnation

I have had the pleasure of meeting at least twelve Marie
Antoinettes, six or seven Marys of Scotland, a whole host of
Louis and other kings, about twenty Great Alexanders, but
never a plain John Smith.

Daniel Dunglas Home

In a useful book for Western readers (1962), Mr Justice
Humphreys, the well-known Buddhist judge, expounds the
view of Theravada Buddhism that the sum of a man's actions –
his *karma* – forms part of his destiny in his next incarnation.
Man is thus 'the moulder and sole creator of his life to come'.
Death itself is seen as a 'well-earned rest' between incarnations
and from this point of view a child may be 'an older pilgrim
than its parents'. Humphreys assesses this doctrine as 'still the
finest moral philosophy extant', and one might be forgiven for
agreeing with him that as a philosophy it has few equals. There
are many phenomena which I should still prefer to interpret in
terms of dissociation, co-consciousness or multiple personality.
I agree with Daniel Dunglas Home that it is just a little
suspicious that one so rarely encounters anyone claiming to
have been just 'a plain John Smith' in a previous incarnation.

I have already referred to the case of Hélène Smith. She was
studied by Theodor Flournoy, Professor of Psychology at the
University of Geneva at the turn of the century, and his book
From India to the Planet Mars (1900) shows how cautiously he too
viewed this colourful lady. 'Hélène Smith' was the pseudonym
of Catherine Müller, a medium who lived in Geneva. She
exhibited what Flournoy himself accepted as multiple secondary personalities. She appears to have been a vivid imager who
also exhibited automatic writing in a number of interesting
forms, some of which she attributed to the spirit of Victor

Hugo. At the time when Flournoy first began to study her, Hélène claimed that in one of her personalities she was the reincarnation of Marie Antoinette; another of her personalities in this 'royal circle' period was her protector Leopold, whom we mentioned earlier. Leopold later identified himself as the shade of Count Cagliostro, alchemist and magician; his writing and voice differed significantly from those of Hélène. The improbability of all this appealed to the investigator, and his doubts increased when the reincarnation of 'Lorenze Feliciana' appeared – this was a fictional character from Alexander Dumas, and not a historical person at all.

In a second phase, Hélène appeared as the reincarnation of the daughter of an Arab chieftain. As 'Simandini' she became a princess by marriage to a Hindu prince; when he died she was burned alive on his funeral pyre. In this previous incarnation, Flournoy himself had been the Indian prince. The third phase was, if possible, even more exotic. Hélène became a person who had been transported to the planet Mars. She gave some interesting descriptions of the landscape, and of the flora and fauna of the planet, and through speech and automatic writing she appeared to have knowledge of a Martian language. In another of her incarnations, Hélène had also been to Uranus; linguistic studies were made of both her 'languages' and they were found to be different – Uranian, it transpired, has some resemblances to French! Hélène later also produced automatic paintings, which do not appear to have been of any great artistic merit.

Various features of this case suggest a strong, somewhat infantile imagination, with many signs of regression. As we have seen, Flournoy chose to interpret Hélène in terms of dissociation and multiple personality. It is unlikely that her fantasies would today be seriously advanced as proof of reincarnation – quite apart from so many other changes since 1900, astronomy is now an experimental science and claims to have visited the planets are subject to other than purely linguistic refutation.

Of particular interest in connection with these out-of-the-body experiences, which are sometimes referred to as 'astral travel', is the phenomenon known to psychology as 'lucid dreams'. These are dreams in which the sleeper knows he is asleep, knows he is dreaming and can exert some control over the dream. The term comes from Frederick van Eeden (1913), who accepts the view that, in sleep, mental functions enter into a state of dissociation. Van Eeden studied 500 of his own dreams, and in 352 of them he had 'full recollection of his daytime life' and was capable of voluntary control. One such lucid dream began with flying and floating; then he saw and talked with his brother, who had died five years before. 'We are dreaming both of us,' said van Eeden. To this his brother replied, 'No, I am not.' In another dream, van Eeden found himself standing at a table near a window. He was perfectly aware that he was dreaming and began to experiment. He tried to break the glass by beating it with a stone. Eventually he succeeded, and threw the broken glass out of the window to see if he could hear it tinkle. He could. He then tried tasting a decanter of wine. While fully aware that he was dreaming, he found that his senses of sight, hearing and taste were functioning quite normally. His 'experimenting' dream also vividly illustrates the power of the dreamer to alter dream events at will. Van Eeden chose to speak of his 'dream body' rather than his 'astral body'. He was clearly aware of a dreamlife body-image with hands, a mouth and other parts, and his lucid dreams were very frequent.

Out-of-the-body experiences have been reported by many people who vigorously reject a supernatural interpretation. A colleague of mine, for example, who is a tough-minded experimentalist with no leanings towards belief in the supernatural, told me that while he was sleeping his 'dream body' seemed to hover about six inches above his sleeping body. He had the impression that he could 'see' both. Such experiences of an out-of-the-body, secondary self can occur outside sleep. Rawcliffe (1959) cites the case of a tank officer whose vehicle was blown up by a landmine: he felt himself floating through the air and looking down at his actual body lying injured below. Depersonalization experiences are familiar to psychiatrists: something very like what we have been describing often occurs under conditions of extreme fatigue or stress. Most of us know what it is like to 'stand outside' what is happening around us, even in very ordinary circumstances; and some people certainly withdraw from themselves under conditions of pain.

Supernatural interpretations of out-of-the-body experiences are very common. In one case, reported in the early 1970s, a certain Sylvan Muldoon claimed that he regularly saw a 'silver cord', slender and glistening, linking his dream body-image with his sleeping self. This silver-cord theme figures prominently in the literature of astral travel. It was regularly reported in a series of cases studied by Crookhill. His subjects tended to feel that their dream self left through the top of the head; it would hover over the body for some time before departure, and a muscular jolting was regularly reported on its return. These out-of-the-body experiences seem to be closely associated with the phenomenon of lucid dreams. One major investigator of these, Mrs Arnold Foster, was regularly troubled by nightmares. She found a solution. When awake she would spend time observing and meditating on the flight of birds. Afterwards she found herself able to increase the frequency of her flying dreams: in awkward nightmare situations she would simply escape by birdlike flight.

Celia Green (1968) reports as one of her illustrations of out-of-the-body experiences the case of a patient in hospital after a minor operation. The patient was 'up near the ceiling watching' two doctors by her own bedside. She seemed detached, and incidentally there is no indication that she herself gave a supernatural interpretation to this experience. By contrast another psychologist colleague of mine *dreamed* that he was in a hospital. The medical staff were talking in hushed tones about some severe condition he seemed to be in. This was an ordinary dream, not a lucid one, but when he woke up he decided to return to the dream and find out what it was all about. He was able, as Bernard Hart has called it (see Chapter 7), to 'gear in', and returned to what was now a lucid dream. In this he actually got out of his dream bed and went over and asked 'what is the matter with me?' His dream companions were reassuring: 'absolutely nothing at all; you are perfectly all right.' He woke up relieved.

A distinction is made by Celia Green between 'lucid dreams' and 'pre-lucid dreams'. In a pre-lucid dream the dreamer will ask himself 'Am I dreaming?' whereas in a lucid dream proper he knows he is asleep. Very many people seem to be familiar with pre-lucid dreams. In one of my own – and others have reported similar experiences – I wondered if I was awake, pinched myself, decided I was and went on dreaming. On one occasion van Eeden, while experiencing a pre-lucid dream, attempted more rigorous tests. During the dream he moistened his finger with saliva and made a wet cross on his left hand. Would it be there when he woke up? He then dreamed that he woke up and verified the presence of the wet cross by applying the wet palm to his cheek. Only after he had really woken up did he discover that his hand had been lying in a closed position undisturbed on his chest during all these dream events. Other tests involved sound. In many of his lucid dreams he would speak loudly, shout and even sing. His wife verified that she had never heard his voice; he had throughout continued to sleep peacefully.

One colleague reported to me considerable puzzlement during one of his dreams. There he was in bed with his wife sleeping beside him. But there was also a dog, a fox terrier, by the bedside. He must be dreaming, as he did not possess a dog. With some difficulty he managed to switch to another mental state: he was in fact asleep, and he woke up. He was able to verify the actuality of the wife, but not of the dog. In full lucid dreams there is no such curiosity about possibly being awake. Celia Green reports one subject who during such a dream was walking along the road with her mother discussing the possibility of lucid dreams. The mother agreed, 'Yes, they are possible.' To this the dreamer replied, 'You realize we are in a dream, now, Mother.' And the mother agreed that, yes, they were. Here is one instance – typical of many – in which the dreamer comments on the dreamlike quality of the dream, but continues to dream.

Most interesting alterations from one kind of mental state to another seem to be involved here. As in multiple personality, one of the sub-systems has knowledge of the other sub-system; functionally, two separate systems are involved, but they have components in common. In some lucid dreams the dreamer may have access to a substantial number of memories relating to past history and ordinary wakefulness. In many respects there are strong analogies here with the co-consciousness of multiple personality in which, as we have seen, one waking sub-system may inflict its thoughts and imagery upon another which the latter experiences as dreams.

Mention has been made of flying experiences in connection with lucid dreams. Very many people spontaneously report flying in their ordinary dreamlife. Flying may also seem to take place in the hypnagogic state. A good description is provided by Leaning (1925) from one of her subjects, Professor Newbold. He had the recurrent hypnagogic experience of 'flying, face downwards, about twenty feet above the ground': 'It is always night and I am following a road, trees, fences, fields dimly seen by the roadside.' Here a distinction may be made between what the individual feels himself to be doing, and what his body actually is doing. Professor Newbold made this distinction. Others have not always done so, particularly those who believe in the occult.

Many nocturnal illusions of flying occur spontaneously without artificial aids. However, in studies reported in 1972 by Michael Harner, dealing with the alleged flight of witches to their sabbaths, there is strong evidence that some ointments used by 'witches' were made from plants containing atropine:

atropine has the two properties of being absorbable through the skin and of creating the impression of flying. In his entertaining book, *Magic: an occult primer* (1972) David Conway provides a number of recipes for the 'do-it-yourself' modern occultist. Two of his 'general purpose' magical oils, whose recipes are included, contain deadly nightshade (belladonna); the second contains henbane as well. Both these botanical substances have atropine in them. A third magical oil, specifically conducive to 'the perception of astral forms', also contains deadly nightshade and henbane. I confess that I have not tried out these substances personally, but if Harner is right then the whole matter of nocturnal flights by those interested in occult practices – whether to sabbaths or elsewhere – becomes less mysterious. Moreover, as many people who reject occult interpretations can also testify, flight in dreams and hypnagogic states may occur quite often spontaneously, without any chemical assistance.

Many individuals, and some whole sections of the world's population, today prefer supernatural explanations to those of naturalistic science. In discussing the 'trance personalities' of the séance room, William McDougall suggests two guiding principles which can be applied to all such phenomena: the Laplace Principle and the Hamlet Principle. The Laplace Principle states that the weight of the evidence should be proportional to the strangeness of the alleged phenomenon. On the whole, in terms of what is scientifically known, it is improbable that I will encounter a ghost or a werewolf on the way home. The evidence that it is not a hallucination, a vivid after-image or a mistaken perception of an Alsatian dog, must be particularly strong. The second principle McDougall names after someone who is no mean example of the psychologist in literature. Nevertheless I prefer to call it the *Horatio* Principle, remembering how Hamlet says to his friend:

> There are more things in heaven and earth, Horatio,
> Than are dreamed of in your philosophy.

The Horatio Principle inspires us to keep our minds open, while the Laplace Principle urges us against suggestibility.

McDougall argues that, in the realm of the apparently supernatural, we need the guidance of both these principles at once, each moderating the other. Certainly the Horatio Principle requires some restraint. Belief, or the wish to believe, in astral dreamlife, possession, ghosts and poltergeists is widespread. We need to admit this wish, examine the evidence, and then accept that the one may be out of proportion to the other. As a mere matter of fact we are often disappointed to learn that a stage magician has produced a supernatural effect by purely natural means. As one such magician said to me, 'People will say, "you did so-and-so". Of course I didn't, it's not possible. But that's what they *think* I did.' Man has a great hunger for magic, and this wish to believe the impossible is very easy to manipulate. Two of my colleagues, Dr Marks and Dr Kammann, who share my preference for the Laplace Principle, are as good as Uri Geller at bending spoons and keys. I believe that their methods – which do not violate the laws of physics, but on the contrary use them – are the same as his.

Marks and Kammann (1978) have also repeated the clairvoyancy experiments of Targ and Puthoff. They failed to find evidence of anything but mental imagery, and this imagery failed to coincide in any way with the target sites which Targ and Puthoff had claimed could be seen through remote viewing. They then examined the original experiments in more detail. There was very strong evidence that the correct 'hits' had been achieved through verbal clues given unwittingly to the subject by the instructions of the experimenter. References might include 'yesterday's two targets', 'nothing like having two successes behind you', 'second place of the day'. Using now only clues of this kind Dr Marks was able to achieve an 100-per-cent correct score, even although he had never visited any of the sites in question.

It is when such marvels as clairvoyant perception of distant places, or the mystery of the 'Bermuda Triangle', are subjected to careful experiments that one becomes sceptical of the Horatio Principle. Not surprisingly, both stage magicians and psychologists are often among the sceptics when faced with miraculous happenings. In the case of the *Hound of the Baskervilles*, Sherlock Holmes himself maintained throughout a purely naturalistic standpoint. His author, Conan Doyle, curiously enough, emerges in his own life as a rather uncritical adherent of the Horatio Principle. He wished to believe. He resisted naturalistic explanations even when the magician Harry Houdini insisted that he had used natural means. Conan Doyle still resisted, even when Houdini explained *how* he did it. Marks and Kammann (1977) encountered similar attitudes to their own Geller-like key-bendings. One of the most powerful methods of scientific investigation of the supernatural is to replicate, and then supply the recipe. When Conan Doyle endorsed 'spirit' photographs as genuine, Houdini showed him how to make similar ones. Magicians like Randi have since repeatedly brought a critically naturalistic standpoint to bear on the supposed supernatural.

Science in general has its labels, and psychology is no exception. Multiple personality, dreams and nightmares, hallucinations, hypnagogic experiences, lucid dreams, co-consciousness – such words may disappoint those who prefer the alternative terminology of the occult. Whichever system our beliefs lead us to adopt, however, there is no doubt that artificial means can be used to increase the frequency and vividness of strange mental events. Upsurges of autonomous visual imagery can be assisted by lack of sleep and sensory deprivation, but there has also been a close association of drugs, particularly hallucinogenic drugs, with occult practices. A good illustration from recent times is to be found in the books of Carlos Castaneda about 'Don Juan', the mysterious American Indian 'man of knowledge' from Mexico. In the course of his instruction in occult matters by this Yaqui Indian sorcerer, Castaneda was given a number of drugs of botanical origin. They included datura, product of the 'devil's weed' *(Datura inoxia)*; psilocybin and other hallucinogens from the mushroom *Psilocybe mexicana*; and mescaline from the peyote cactus *(Lophophoria williamsii)*. These are all very potent substances. Probably more than one active principle was involved in each: there is all the difference in the world between 'pure', scientifically synthetic mescaline or psilocybin, and raw materials from the plants themselves.

There is a substantial scientific literature on the hallucinogens and their psychological effects. On the whole it is an upsurge of vivid and highly autonomous visual imagery rather than 'hallucination' that is reported. From experiments we did in the mid 1950s at Aberdeen Medical School, I am myself familiar with mescaline. On the first of several occasions when mescaline was administered to me, I sought to communicate with the experimenters about the imagery. I referred to, indeed seized upon, its resemblances to visual hypnagogic imagery. Later we discovered that very many other investigators had, quite independently, noted this strong resemblance. The imagery seems to surge up from some place other than one's usual self: from somewhere resembling Enid Blyton's 'under-mind'. Like hypnagogic imagery it may be very beautiful, and its lighting and colour may have an unearthly quality. Again, like hypnagogic imagery, it may exhibit microscopic detail, and the strangest combinations of objects, familiar or unfamiliar. Our subjects found themselves unable to control its flow: very often they were absorbed in the imagery and wanted to disregard the efforts of the experimenters to elicit and score responses. These experimenters often received rather scornful treatment as though from a kind of mystical 'on high'. Some of our subjects made lofty utterances on such topics as 'Reality', 'Truth', and 'The Nature of Time'. During one time-estimation task one subject complained that the experimenters had left his watch on his wrist; but *he* didn't mind, since what he was interested in was, 'Time' rather than 'time'.

In one of his most famous metaphors, the Greek philosopher Plato conceived of man as chained in a cave, aware only of the shadows of real objects. This idea seems to appeal to subjects under mescaline and other such drugs. The subject may have the strong impression that the 'Veil of Maya', which ordinarily obscures the realm of 'Reality' behind mere appearance, has been drawn back. In the liberation he now feels he may express in a grandiose and mystical way the inadequacy of mere words to convey his sense of wonder. The subject may feel himself transported to some other world, the world of Plato's Forms, or Jung's Archetypes. All this can be somewhat tiresome for the experimenters; but such psychological happenings, and the deep sense of significance that accompanies them, accord closely with supernatural, mystical and occult belief systems, so they must be studied. Their connection with mystical thinking is obvious; their validity in any other than a religious sense is a matter on which opinion will be divided.

Jung has pointed out repeatedly, and with emphasis, that the men of the West have much to learn from the men of the East. He stresses the importance of waking and sleeping imagery. He paid careful attention to his own dreams, and regarded them as a helpful guide to the solution of his waking problems. A striking lesson in these matters is provided by the work of Kilton Stewart (Tart, ed., 1969). Stewart made studies of the Senoi people of the Malay peninsula. These isolated jungle people make systematic use of dream interpretations in their children's education. Stewart comments that 'breakfast in a Senoi house is like a dream clinic'. The parents will systematically discuss their children's dreams, reassure their anxieties and fears and encourage the young to learn from them. More than most Westerners they recognize that dreams reflect the preoccupations and problems of the wakeful state. As Stewart points out, we tend to neglect this aspect of inner experience. The seemingly primitive Senoi have much to teach us. They choose not to interpret their dreaming and hypnagogic experiences as demonic possession and have advanced beyond such superstitious beliefs. In their different ways both Jung and the Senoi advocate acceptance and self-knowledge, not only of the conscious self, but of sub-systems of the personality beyond it. Perhaps some of the literature of the occult (including the uses of hallucinogenic drugs in the 'Don Juan' tradition) should be re-interpreted in these terms.

It is exceedingly hard to step outside the parochial assumptions of one's own culture. These tempt us at every point. To illustrate, some years ago I heard a debate in Scotland on 'whether a religious revival would be a good thing'. Late in the debate a member of the audience spoke from the floor. He was a Moslem. He drew attention to the millions of people of his own religious faith in the world, and asked the audience whether they were quite sure they wanted a Moslem religious revival. Up till then nobody had thought of this. The debate had proceeded in a parochial way on the assumption 'religion = Christian religion'. Men of the East can make similar culture-bound mistakes. The Tibetan, Dawa Norbu (1974), gives an account of the arrival of a group of Chinese soldiers, enthusiastic about 'liberating Tibet'. They encountered a small team of Tibetan labourers, who began to clap their hands. This delighted the Chinese, as evidence of the warmth of their welcome. Only later did they discover their error. The most effective ritual that a Tibetan can use against unwelcome intruders is to clap the hands and curse simultaneously. This was precisely what they were doing. But the invaders mistook the nature of the action, within the rigidity of their own cultural frame of reference.

Attempts to 'educate' people of another culture to accept one's own cultural frame of reference can misfire badly. A striking illustration is reported by Marvin Harris (1975). It involved a rather troublesome prophet from a remote part of New Guinea. In the mid 1940s the Australian government decided to cope with this man, Yali, by taking him to Australia and showing him its wonders. So Yali was escorted around aircraft factories, and shown roads and tall buildings. But what impressed him most were two things: the Queensland Museum and the Brisbane Zoo. There in the museum he found many familiar objects from New Guinea. These included the ritual masks which missionaries had tried to convince his people were 'works of Satan'. Now he knew otherwise: such things were preserved, with obvious reverence, in glass cases; they were attended by priests in white gowns, and worshipped by well-to-do people who came and always spoke in respect-fully hushed tones in their presence. These impressions were confirmed by Yali's experiences at the Brisbane Zoo. Here he found many familiar animals, and some new ones, all carefully looked after. He also discovered that many Australians kept cats and dogs, which were accorded privileged treatment. The truth finally dawned upon him when he was shown illustra-tions in a book. These showed apes and monkeys becoming progressively similar to man. He had been taught by the missionaries that Adam and Eve were man's ancestors. Now he knew that the white man really believed that his ancestors were monkeys, cats, dogs and other animals. And this was what Yali's own people had believed, before the white mis-sionaries had tricked them into giving up their totems.

Given how widely belief systems vary, it seems unavoidable that from culture to culture, and even from individual to individual, mental states will be interpreted in widely different ways. Religion, philosophy, superstition, science, literature and the prevailing social order will all play their part in shap-ing our view of our inner lives. Am I hallucinating, or do I simply have a vivid imagination? Is it an evil spirit, an appari-tion, a previous incarnation? Is it an outside power speaking through me, or a sub-system of my own personality? And *why*? Imagination imagery is a strange and wonderful thing, as we shall continue to see in the next chapter. People vary enorm-ously in the range and intensity of their mental imagery: some have vivid images as their constant companions, others claim never to have 'had' an image at all!

6
Imagination and Imagery

I shut my eyes for a few minutes with my portable typewriter on my knee . . . my characters stand before me in my mind's eye . . . as if I had a private cinema screen there.

Enid Blyton

In everyday waking life, imagery – visual, auditory or of some other kind – may be an important component of our thinking, remembering and imagining. Some people assert that their imagery is vivid, rich and interesting. Others declare that they barely know the meaning of the word. A certain academic of my acquaintance, D.C., lost his entire collection of slides taken during a trip to Europe: he told me that he might just as well never have gone on that holiday, since nothing of what he had seen was recorded visually in his memory. I asked him to close his eyes and describe his wife. He was completely unable to give any description of her appearance. His mind's eye was 'blind'. Another man who closely resembled D.C. told me that he had only recently begun to understand what other people meant when they told him about being able to 'look back' over their recent holidays; he felt that he was missing out considerably.

We have seen how Robert Louis Stevenson used dream imagery in his creative writings: his imagery would 'labour all night long . . . making stories for the market'. Enid Blyton, in her stories for children, would make similar use of her imagery while fully awake. This autonomous imagery, which was visual as well as auditory, she likened to 'a private cinema screen'. She accepted the imagery from what she called her 'under-mind' in wholly naturalistic terms, believing that it stemmed from past perception of her own. In a series of letters to me, written during the years 1953–57 (the principal letters appear

81

as an appendix to the authorized biography by Stoney, 1974), she explained that she could 'both write a story and read it at the same moment of time'. The letters talk of the entertaining nature of her imagery and its often unexpected forms:

> To write book after book without knowing what is to be said or done sounds silly, and yet it happens. Sometimes a character makes a joke, a really funny one that makes me laugh as I type it on my paper – and I think 'Well, I couldn't have thought of that myself in a hundred years!' And then I think, 'Well, *who* did think of it then?'

In the case of Enid Blyton what we are seeing, according to my frame of reference, is a sub-system of the personality – remote from the ego or self system – providing upsurges of imagery into the consciousness. Morton Prince has likened the sensation to putting one's hand into someone else's pocket and drawing out objects 'not one's own'. Enid Blyton is an extreme example, but many of us experience something very similar in the imagery of our ordinary dreams.

A distinction can be made between two sorts of mental imagery: the one is subject to voluntary control, the other is not. In *controlled imagery* the author is able to summon up images, then modify or dismiss them at will. By contrast, *autonomous imagery* seems to enjoy a life of its own: the imager himself feels like a spectator. Autonomous imagery is common in dreaming, in its usual forms; it is also characteristic of the hypnagogic state; and, as we have seen in such cases as Miss Blyton's, it may play its part in the creative thinking of wakefulness. Writers provide abundant illustration of such imagery which, as Wordsworth says, can 'flash upon that inward eye, which is the bliss of solitude'. Wordsworth talks of vivid imagery 'dazzling the vision that presumes to gaze', and he refers to in inward eye creating 'a landscape more august than happiest skill of pencil ever clothed'. Unlike Enid Blyton, some writers have made a living from descriptive writing without any support from autonomous imagery. A striking instance is an author whom I shall call J.D.

His knowledge of imagery comes largely from dreams and is mostly absent from his waking life. The method he uses – and he has written many highly successful paperback novels – involves much use of the camera. He will go to a country, choose a suitable area and take numerous photographs. Then he will settle down with his collection of slides and develop the atmosphere for his story by projecting and studying them in their full colour.

Along with Enid Blyton and J.D. may be mentioned a third author, and his imagery. Charles Hamilton – best-known to many as 'Frank Richards', who created the fat boy, Billy Bunter – was a prolific writer of the controlled-imagery type. He wrote under as many as four different pseudonyms and put his vivid visual and auditory imagery to some ingenious uses. During meetings with one rather boringly talkative publisher, for example, he would, while appearing to be listening, 'play' music to himself (Skilton 1962). Sometimes he would sub-vocally recite. On occasions he would resort to chess-playing and the dialogue (with Hamilton's own contribution inaudible) would run like this:

Publisher: I've got an idea for the title of a story . . .
Hamilton: Pawn to king's fourth – pawn to king's fourth.
Publisher: I think it's rather a good title . . .
Hamilton: Pawn to king's bishop's fourth; queen to rook's fourth: check . . .

Hamilton played these chess games with himself, while the garrulous publisher remained wholly unaware of the contest between Frank's various chess-playing sub-systems. Many of us have played chess with ourselves, but Hamilton seems to have developed this skill to a high degree, and a flight from the pressure of external events and boredom. The number of his pseudonyms is remarkable, and even when Hamilton wrote autobiographically he did so in a curiously impersonal way: his writing is in the third person, and always about 'Frank', never 'I'. For the most part one might tend to link minor forms of dissociation with autonomous rather than well-controlled imagery: 'Frank Richards' represents an interesting exception.

In discussing imagery in its relations to creative thought I have found it useful to distinguish authorship and editorship. Imagery, whether waking, sleeping or hypnagogic, may provide the raw materials, but some editing process may need to follow. After the dream which provided the nucleus of *Dr Jekyll and Mr Hyde*, Stevenson spent six weeks polishing up the story; many other writers have needed hard 'editorial' revision to transform the imagery, dream or reverie into a useful work of art. Some writers like Enid Blyton found 'authorship' easy. Others like Émile Zola found it hard. Zola would actually resort to the device of writing letters to himself about his characters as a way of tuning in on his authorship processes. Perhaps Voltaire meant it literally and was referring to the same tendencies in himself when he wrote, 'Criticism is easy, art is difficult'. On one well-known occasion Dr Johnson helped the impecunious Oliver Goldsmith to settle down to editing his unpolished material; from this emerged *The Vicar of Wakefield*. To a large extent, 'editorship' can be accomplished by the writer himself, working on the fruits of his own authorship processes: two different functions within the same personality.

Elsewhere I have coined the term 'imagery parochialism' to describe the peculiar blindness people may exhibit to the possibility that others may differ from themselves in their imagery. As the psychologist T. H. Pear put it, 'some people write as though everybody were a visualizer, or *ought* to be'. Many of my subjects have told me of the ridicule they experienced, particularly as children, when they were unwise enough to admit to some innocent variant of their image life. Many have pondered thoughtfully over their own. One young woman with a capacity for crystal-gazing imagery wrote to me: 'It's funny, that "surely everybody thinks like me" feeling . . . it does cause quite a shock sometimes to find that *nobody* in one's immediate environment does.' One correspondent spoke eloquently of the emotional and psychological distress that this realization can cause. Her own variant was changes in her body-image, which occurred both hypnagogically and in full wakefulness, in her childhood. She wrote: 'it is terrifying enough for a small child to face alone in the dark . . . but when one is only five . . . in a bus and people are looking . . . one learned to keep a dead-pan face, and to study one's bus ticket in one elephant-sized hand, but I always thought it was the onset of madness.' It is a help that names exist; the labelling of such experiences as body-image changes, *déjà vu*, hypnagogic and hypnopompic imagery can at least reassure us that we are not unique.

It is a gross over-simplification to assess imagery variations merely by distinguishing 'visiles', 'audiles' and 'motiles'. To begin with, a given individual may rely largely on his visual

RANGE OF MENTAL IMAGERY

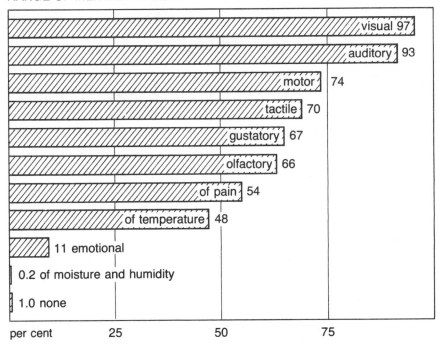

			visual 97
			auditory 93
		motor 74	
		tactile 70	
	gustatory 67		
	olfactory 66		
	of pain 54		
of temperature 48			
11 emotional			
0.2 of moisture and humidity			
1.0 none			

per cent   25   50   75

Results of asking 500 people to report on the types of mental imagery available to them in their thinking, remembering and imagining.

imagery in thought and memory, but also have access to auditory, motor, tactile and other imagery of reasonable strength. We have perhaps also been unduly concerned with mere strength of imagery rather than with the range and richness of inter-connection between different imagery modes. An investigation of my own will serve to illustrate three main areas of imagery variation. The subjects were 500 adults from a wide range of different occupations. First I asked them about their *predominant type* of imagery. The majority reported that they relied predominantly upon visual imagery, with auditory imagery a poor second; but in the case of memory it was frequently found that a combination of visual and auditory imagery was at work. I then investigated *range* of imagery. The subjects revealed an unexpectedly wide repertoire of image modes: more than half of them reported image-experience in as many as seven of the senses – movement, touch, taste, smell and awareness of pain as well as sight and hearing – and nearly half had imagery of temperature as well. Finally I questioned the *strength* of their imagery: in which modes did they have reasonably strong imagery? Reasonable strength is an imprecise measurement, but it was interesting nonetheless that 86 per cent claimed reasonably strong visual imagery and 69 per cent claimed reasonably strong auditory imagery (McKellar 1965, 1977).

These findings can enable us to make more sophisticated distinctions. One man, for example, might be predominantly a visualizer; but he might have access also to six or seven other modes of imagery, with reasonably strong imagery for, say, taste and smell along with vision and hearing. Another individual's predominant imagery might be auditory; but this might be his only mode of imagery, and furthermore it might be weak and fragmentary. Imagery may be composite: a person may visualize a scene, have accompanying auditory imagery of people talking, and be able to image also the warmth of the sunshine. Some people may be low-powered in one area, but strong in others. The late Sir Cyril Burt described his own thinking as 'like a broadcast debate', with auditory imagery (lacking visual accompaniments) of people's voices 'arguing together in the twilight'. One of my present psychologist colleagues describes himself as similarly without visual imagery: he doesn't even dream visually. He told me that he 'had a visual dream once when I was about 5 years old'! He was prepared to admit that other people's mental life differed from his own.

These variations of imagery experience have considerable bearing on both labels and interpretations. At first sight it might be thought that those who report auditory hallucinations will tend to be strong auditory imagers. This does not appear to be the case. In one important study in 1947 Seitz and Molholm discovered that the auditory imagery of patients reporting auditory hallucinations was markedly weaker than that of patients not reporting them. In a parallel study they discovered that visually hallucinated patients tended, similarly, to be low-powered rather than high-powered visual imagers. There is sense in this apparent paradox. We establish our frame of reference towards a subject from familiarity with it; it is the unfamiliar and unusual that gives us trouble. As one of my own subjects once put it to me: 'I've had a visual image once or twice. They nearly frightened me out of my wits.' The person familiar with visualization in his thought and memory is much less likely to interpret such phenomena as supernatural 'visions' or hallucinations.

Each of us has to be able to come to terms with the behaviour of his sleeping mind at least as much as, if not more than, of his waking mind. Much has been written about sleep and dreams, and many of us know how active the imagination can be both in the drowsy state before sleep and in the moments of waking. One subject of my investigations reported an experience which illustrates once again how unreliable our judgments can be as to whether we are asleep at all. He was in bed asleep, and woke to find himself standing in a bath. Although it was a normal bath he was disturbed to notice that his head only came up to the rim of the tub. He opened his eyes widely and said to himself 'I am conscious', and then proceeded to experiment. He bounced up and down several times in slow motion, and then began to notice shapes appearing on the sides of the bath. These he assured himself were hypnagogic images, such as he experienced regularly. At this point, he 'woke up' for the second time. On waking he had full memory for these dream events, but he seemed also to have acquired the ability to fly: he tried 'two backward flips which were successful. As I was landing from my second flip the four-year-old girl who lives in the house came into my room.' At this point he 'woke up', for the third time. He recalled his experience of flying with some pleasure, and went into the kitchen to have breakfast. On the table he found an unusually elaborate meal of meat and potatoes. He left for the bathroom, and it was only then that he woke up properly. Experiences of this kind are by no means uncommon, although this is the only case I have encountered in which false wakenings were three deep. As Havelock Ellis said in *The World of Dreams* (1911), 'dreams are true while they last'.

Freud has some interesting things to say about the protective function of dreams. One of the dreams he discussed concerned a young medical student, Herr Pepi. On the occasion concerned, Pepi was dreaming peacefully when his landlady called to him: it was time for him to get up and go to the hospital where he worked. The protective function of dreaming intervened. Pepi proceeded to dream that in the hospital there was a bed, carrying a notice which read 'Herr Pepi, Occupation Medical Student'. He had found a fantasy solution to the problem of getting up to go to work: if he was in bed in the hospital ward there was no need for him to get up and go there. In the meanwhile he was able to snatch a few more moments of sleep. Freud himself labels the experience a dream. In my own studies of hypnopompic imagery I have found many such cases. The person concerned will 'wake up', 'get out of bed', 'wash and dress' and then discover that he is still in bed dozing

and will have to perform these actions all over again. Drawing
the line between dreaming and such hypnopompic imaging is
sometimes extremely difficult.

Numerous confusions of imagery experiences with real
events occur in these states which divide full wakefulness and
sleep. In their typical forms both hypnagogic and hypnopompic imagery are, like dream imagery, characteristically
autonomous. The would-be sleeper may be roused from his
dozing by the telephone, the music of a radio or the sound of a
doorbell. Many of my own subjects have got up from bed to
take appropriate action, only to discover that these sounds
were purely hypnagogic. Hypnagogic music and hypnagogic
voices seem to be particularly common. Not uncommon also
are the false intrusions in the early morning of hypnopompic
alarm clocks and calls to wakefulness.

Hypnagogic imagery usually takes the form of strange sequences of images of brief duration, but on occasions it may
assume a longer, more narrative form. Such narratives have a
plot of their own, a plot in which the imager may find himself
participating without any sense of authorship. A measure of
limited control is sometimes to be found. One hypnagogic
imager told me that he could on occasion 'step into the play as
an actor might walk on to the state'. He was then able to 'act
the part of a magician and transform the action, even change
the characters'. He added that, afterwards, 'my play proceeds
normally'. The same kind of relationship operates in full sleep,
in 'lucid dreams'; in these the dreamer knows he is asleep and
has considerable control over the dream events. But generally,
in both dreams and hypnagogic imagery, even such limited
control is not possible.

One hypnagogic imager told me that he has the experience
more or less nightly. He explained, 'I get a lot of landscapes . . .
the scene is going on of its own accord, but I can put something
in.' He gave an example: 'I can't say "I'll have a square
cloud", but I can say "I'd like a different one, thanks". And a
different one will come. You can't specify.' (Note his grateful

'thanks' to his obliging undermind!) For the most part it is tempting to see hypnagogic imagery as 'something from outside'. Certainly it is outside the voluntary intentions and waking consciousness of the would-be sleeper, and as such it appears as a kind of invasion from the dreamworld. Very many people have chosen to give it occult or supernatural interpretations in terms of an 'astral realm' or of visions of an 'afterlife'. One such imager told me that as a child he had believed that the imagery came from seeing through the eyes of another person – somebody on the other, lighted, side of the world.

We have seen how Enid Blyton was sometimes surprised and amused by the creative products of her undermind. Dreams can indeed be entertaining, but many of us have been frightened too. My own hypnagogic imagery has even provoked righteous indignation (remember how provocative the teasing Sally Beauchamp was in Morton Prince's famous case). On one such occasion a group of people were standing around when suddenly a stranger emerged who proceeded to shoot them down. Although it was a product of my own mental life, I was quite indignant about the whole affair. It was a wholly unprovoked attack upon innocent people, within my internal society. Another common reaction to autonomous hypnagogic imagery is embarrassment. One imager saw himself setting off to a fancy-dress party. He was wearing the mask of Winnie the Pooh's friend Piglet. In this hypnagogically imaged episode he found himself greeted at the door by a stern official. This man said nothing; he merely pointed to a notice which read: 'The management reserves the right to refuse admission.' The implication was clear: 'You are unwelcome. No pigs allowed in here.' A teasing sub-system of my correspondent's personality – a Sally or an amused Eve Black – was having a good time discomforting the more prim, more conscious self.

In controlled imagery we encounter some ingenious uses, but there is the same crucial difference between the relatively harmless and the harmful. It seems that imagery of both kinds can be used as an avoidance-technique, to postpone/distract our attention from/avoid the issue of something tedious or unpleasant – the danger being quite simply that we may not know when to stop. We have seen how some writers have had cause to be grateful for upsurges of imagery, controlled or autonomous, in their waking as in their sleeping lives. We have also seen some examples of the less enchanting influence of the dissociated mind. In this context of risk it is worth looking at athletes for a moment.

Psychologists have observed among athletes a phenomenon referred to as 'mental practice', which can have some effect on final performance. William Morgan's study of marathon runners (1978) indicates that imagery can also be used as a way of coping with boredom or pain. One runner used to 'listen to' Beethoven. Another reported that in the early stages of a race he would look around at the landscape and the other runners, but after about fifteen miles he would escape into imagery. He would imagine himself in his study, and proceed to design a house. After 'designing' it he would proceed to 'construct' it, labouring at building, electrical wiring and plumbing. If at the end of all this there was still further to run, he would go back to his desk and improve the design. One woman athlete made use of her feelings to spur herself on: she would image the faces of people she detested and proceed to 'step on' these faces for the next twenty-six miles! Several other runners reported a tendency to review their lives or escape into childhood. One of these would imagine himself back with his father in a locomotive engine. His body would become changed into the engine itself, his legs would become powerful pistons and he would negotiate the next hill 'with relative ease'.

William Morgan himself uses the term 'dissociation' for this switching of attention away from demands upon the body to the relief or stimulus of imaginative imagery. This behaviour amongst athletes is not so very different from the escape-attempts made by many of us from psychological rather than physical pressures. People like Sybil are a sad warning of the dangers of psychological escape, conscious or unconscious, but the rare condition of 'pain-blindness' may serve to emphasize that there can be similar dangers in too successful an escape from physical pressures. The 'pain-blind' person runs quite terrifying risks of bodily harm, since, for example, he would not necessarily know if his own body was on fire. Dissociative behaviour has its uses, but we are beginning to see that it can be taken too far, even in everyday life.

7

Sleep and
Its Adjacent States

The principal impression produced upon the waking mind in
the morning . . . [is] of something alien, arising from another
world, and contrasting with the remaining contents of the
mind.

Sigmund Freud

With the interesting exception of lucid dreams, we are confined
to retrospective study of our dream life. By contrast the
dream-*like* imagery of the hypnagogic state permits introspection at the time of its occurrence, and the hypnagogic imager
can even sound-record his imagery. (As someone who has and
remembers occasional hypnagogic imagery, I have done this
myself.) The regular imager has a head-start in understanding
what is going on, and in this chapter I shall be drawing heavily
upon the experiences of two in particular, whom I have called
R.G. and P.S. They have made detailed records of their hypnagogic imagery; they have drawn and painted the imagery;
they have sound-recorded it. We have had detailed discussions
of these introspections in terms of my own interest in these
phenomena over many years (McKellar and Simpson 1954),
and it is my belief that hypnagogic imagery may assist us
considerably in our study of the minor dissociative phenomena
of normal mental life.,

P.S., who has visual hypnagogic imagery more or less
nightly, made an interesting tape-recording relating to the
threshold between sleep and the hypnagogic state. His image
on this occasion was of a cliff with a cave in it. Hypnagogic
images often appear in microscopic detail, and P.S. 'zoomed
in' on the cave to study this. He then reported to the tape-

recorder (in this instance in retrospect) that the image was 'lost all together – unfortunately I dropped off to sleep then.' His sleep lasted roughly a quarter of an hour. He continued:

> This strange half-awake, half-asleep state – where I was having lapses of consciousness and wasn't aware of things. It seemed that I was probably dreaming, and that I came to from a dream. I was carrying over things that I had been dreaming about . . . a state of oscillating between half-consciousness and unconsciousness and it became hard to differentiate between what is hypnagogic image and what is dream.

At this point the recording stopped, and sleep ensued.

P.S.'s reference to 'oscillating' in the hypnagogic state is of some interest: on the one hand the system of waking consciousness, on the other the dreaming system, with a fragile hypnagogic bridge between them. Memory may or may not take part. As that acute introspectionist Sally Beauchamp reported, much more imagery goes on than we remember, and it is only what we remember that we call 'dreams'. On waking we are often aware of just having lost a dream: it eludes our recall. But it has not necessarily gone for ever. In a drowsy state, with eyes closed, if we can elude perceptual interruption from outside, we may be able to recall the dream sequence. For my own part I can sometimes still remember one act of the sequence, and on occasion even two or three. But too often the amnesic walls between the sleeping sequences and the events of waking up are absolute.

In our first investigation of hypnagogic phenomena in 1954, Lorna Simpson and I distinguished two types. Both exhibited a high degree of autonomy. We named these types 'perservative' and 'impersonal':

Perservative Imagery
The perceptual origins are obvious. Imagery relates to recent events. Examples include visual 'perseverations' of fruit-picking or microscopic work, and motor 'perseverations' of skating, tennis or some other sporting activity.

Impersonal Imagery

No clear relation to previous perception. Subjects often likened such imagery to surrealist paintings, remarking on clarity of detail, oddity of content, and juxtapositions of familiar with unfamiliar objects. Such imagery seems creative rather than merely reproductive, and strangely foreign to one's own mental life.

Some hypnagogic imagers seem to be confined to perseverative imagery, which in its visual forms can be provoked by visual fatigue, as after driving or fruit-picking. In my own case I find that after weeding my garden I go on 'seeing' weeds. Those who weed by species may find that one weed, and that one alone, will perseverate hypnagogically. Recently I did a 'mixed' weeding. That night I had a veritable hypnagogic botany lesson on the weeds of a New Zealand garden. They were all there, docks, dandelions, convolvulus roots, and several more which I could not name although I had been dealing sternly with them all afternoon. I had not, myself, consciously decided on this review of the afternoon's events, but – like the typical hypnagogic imager – I watched the performance with interest.

Impersonal hypnagogic imagery, in its visual forms, is of considerable interest. It involves scenes and events that do not seem to belong to one's own mental life at all. Two of my subjects gave graphic descriptions of this second type of imagery. One said it was 'like scenes from the kind of travel books I don't read'. The second likened it to 'a succession of vivid lantern slides, occurring without warning, and containing detailed information which I didn't know I knew'. Yet another subject reported his imagery as follows: Bay scene, pale blue-white sea, cliff and face with very detailed and beautiful rock, with iron railing on top. Semi-silhouette 'of two prehistoric animals walking in what would be a public observation area . . .' In this case the subject was able to locate the seascape as one familiar to him – although it was not one usually adorned

95

with prehistoric animals. The landscapes of hypnagogic imagery are rarely of familiar places. The Frenchman Alfred Maury (who provided the label 'hypnagogic imagery') often saw faces, too, and they were invariably of people unfamiliar to him, with strange and bizarre hair-styles. Many subjects give similar reports. We seem seldom to meet people we know, or visit familiar places, in the strange world of hypnagogic imaging. The attractions of a supernatural interpretation are obvious.

The range of this imagery, and its odd sequences, can be very striking. Note the following, 'seen from above': 'A staircase of string in space. A bald, pale-skinned Indian rides a bicycle down staircase, wearing white tennis shorts . . .' The imagery is often hugely entertaining: one of my earlier subjects had a kind of imagery cartoon-show more or less nightly. A more recent subject reported a snowscape 'washed in white' across which a group of snowmen were proceeding; each had in his hand a Christmas tree with an umbrella-shaped handle. The imager liked that. 'It was really jolly,' he told me. The kind of waking imagery which so amused Enid Blyton is quite familiar to the hypnagogic imager. One reported seeing 'a dachshund dog dressed in a tartan coat with breeches and a puppy dressed the same . . . it was very amusing . . . they were dancing'. This same subject described her regular hypnagogic imagery as straight out of Walt Disney's *Jungle Book*, including in one instance a sabre-toothed tiger; she knew there was no such tiger either in the original Kipling story or in the Walt Disney film, but it was there – 'it is like a joke worked out for my entertainment'.

The emotional reponse to hypnagogic imaging varies enormously, and some of the most hair-raising visions can be watched by the imager with surprising detachment. Images are not always entertaining, however, was we have seen, and in certain circumstances 'faces in the dark' will terrify. As one such subject put it, sometimes the imagery is 'too vivid, and too extraordinarily evil, not to belong to something real, somewhere'. One psychologist told me that hypnagogic imagery for her was like a kind of nightmare which she had to work through before sleep would come. So much depends on our current mental state, and on the beliefs surrounding us. In an appropriate environment it is easy to see how vivid hypnagogic imagery would fit in with, or provoke, beliefs about evil spirits seeking to invade or possess the personality.

For the most part, it seems, the hypnagogic imager does not himself participate in the imagery. There are a few exceptions. In one hypnagogic nightmare the subject found himself part of a flock of sheep standing outside a slaughter yard. 'I was one of them,' he said. 'We moved up the gangway. I could feel what all the sheep felt like.' Before the image faded he saw the slaughter-man's face, and the expression it held. He found the experience exceptionally frightening. (It is interesting that this hypnagogic sequence ended outside the slaughterhouse: in his waking life, which had provided the raw material for the nightmare, the subject was familiar with slaughterhouses, but only from the outside.) Such 'autoscopic' imagery, imagery of oneself, is common in waking life, but on the whole it seems to be a rarity in the hypnagogic state.

Dreams themselves generally seem to reflect the interests, sentiments and emotional preoccupations of the dreamer rather more clearly than do these curious upsurges of imagery in the hypnagogic state – but as many of us know, they can play quite whimsically upon our problems. I found myself once at loggerheads during a Faculty meeting with a senior member of my university for whom I have a high respect. It so happens that he smokes. That night in my dream I found myself sitting down and writing out, on small pieces of paper, all that I thought was wrong with the university. I stuffed the pieces of paper into the bowl of a pipe and handed it to my colleague. It was a perfect expression of 'you can put this in your pipe and smoke it'!

My favourite example of this autonomous sense of humour in our dreamlife concerns a mathematician friend. At the time he was working furiously on a doctoral thesis on the mathematics of gravitation, and he had had to give up for the time being thinking about anything else at all. One night he dreamed that he was a trapeze artist at a circus. He fell. Fortunately his dream body was secured by a safety rope which caught him inches before he would have hit the ground, and there he hung, upside down. While thus suspended, he was approached by a pretty girl with a tray of the chocolates she was selling. The discomforted mathematician could only say to her, 'I'm sorry I can do nothing for you. I'm hung up on gravitation.' His Ph.D. examination was, I am happy to report, successful.

This function of dreaming as an expression of the problems of our waking selves was explored by Dostoevsky. It was studied in detail by Freud, who developed a profound understanding of the continuity of our waking and our sleeping minds. Herbert Silberer regarded hypnagogic imaging in similar terms: such imaging provides a more concrete expression, sometimes even in cartoon-like form, of our preoccupations. *Conflict and Dream*, by W. H. R. Rivers, developed this view. Like other forms of imaging, however autonomous, dreaming presents no particular mystery. It comprises a 'living over', and a working through, in the altered mental state of sleep, of the issues that concern and interest our waking selves. The emotional tone of the dream depends on how successfully we achieve a fantasy solution to these problems. If we are successful we are likely to have a pleasant wish-fulfilment dream; if unsuccessful, there will result an anxiety dream, or in extreme cases a nightmare. I have found that this formula fits the dreams I have encountered, in myself, in other people and in the research literature. Rivers and Silberer between them admit that our problem-solving processes operate at a more primitive level in dreams and hypnagogic imaging than in everyday life. As Silberer puts it, 'the tired consciousness . . . switches to an easier level of mental functioning'.

Dreams and hypnagogic imagery can make extraordinarily apt observations – sometimes expressing satisfactorily more than one problem at once. The following dream occurred not once but twice to a friend, during the same night. In the dream she saw a blackboard, attached to which was an unusual sort of poster, made of a botanical leaf. This leaf was held to the blackboard by the paws, and claws, of some animal. On the leaf-poster, held by these cat-like paws, were a series of messages, written in the form of a series of questions as in an advertisement:

ARE YOUR ANIMALS TROUBLING YOU?
ARE THEY NEUROTIC?
ARE THEY OFF THEIR FOOD?
If so, send them to us, and we will cure them for you.

Then followed the address of some organization. The free associations which I obtained from this dream are revealing. During the day in question, tenants had left the dreamer's downstairs flat: she hoped they had taken their three cats with them! More generally, the dreamer had had frequent cause recently to use the word 'cat' about a certain female acquaintance of hers. The dream encapsulated her problem most ingeniously. *Somewhere*, she hoped, was a friendly organization prepared to give therapy – and a home – to troublesome creatures.

It is worth comparing artificially induced altered mental states with those of normal sleep. Hypnosis and the hypnotic state will be discussed in the next chapter, so let us look for a moment here at some interesting conditions produced by general anaesthetic, which have engaged much recent research interest. Vivid dreams may occur under anaesthetics. A certain colleague (whose introspections I trust) tells me that during dental extraction he dreamed of a swordfish diving straight towards him. He was sure that he felt the extraction of the tooth in the tearing of his flesh by the swordfish. There is naturally some anxiety in medical circles generally that patients under general anaesthetic may be consciously aware of such pain, and of other events during operations. The

surgeon J. E. Utting in 1975 recorded that he personally interviewed more than thirty patients who 'claimed they were
conscious when they were supposed to be anaesthetized'. Half
of these reported feeling pain. These sensations were sometimes accompanied by dream imagery. One of Utting's sam-
ple, who was having a major abdominal operation, dreamed
that he was at a fairground and that somebody was throwing
knives at his stomach. Such dreamlife may extend into the
waking-up period, and blend with reality. I myself recall a
vivid hypnopompic experience, after a dental extraction. I
awoke to find my dentist standing there in the middle of a
stream, wearing waders and otherwise equipped as a trout
fisherman.

Out-of-the-body experiences are also reported in the altered
mental states accompanying anaesthesia. In a letter to *The
Lancet* (16 March 1974) Shackleton tells of a patient under
ether who had reported that she felt herself to be some feet
above the operating theatre. She claimed to have experienced
'no fear, merely interest' in what was happening to herself, and
was also able to give a reasonably accurate account of the
spatial positions of the various people in the room. Renewed
interest in anaesthetic phenomena has incidentally confirmed
existing strong evidence that people dream more often than
was originally suspected. The distinction now, as we saw
earlier, is rather between recallers and non-recallers than between dreamers and non-dreamers. Furthermore, Brice and
colleagues (1970) found that anaesthetic dreaming was far
more often reported where patients were asked about it as soon
as they woke up than if the question was left until later.

The hypnagogic imager – whose great advantage is that he
can see what is happening – functions as two systems. One part
of him observes what the other part chooses to show him on his
personal cinema screen. William James wrote of dissociation in
terms of 'systems thrown out of gear with each other' (1890).
Bernard Hart later produced the same metaphor, when he
talked of dissociation as less an affair of 'splitting', and more a

matter of 'gearing'. He wrote of 'an affair of gearing, the various elements of mental machinery being organized into different functional systems by throwing in of the appropriate gear' (1939). This analogy of a change of gear between different systems seems introspectively appropriate to both dreaming and the hypnagogic state. The operation of two such systems seems particularly evident, however, in the hypnagogic case. One regular imager reported in interview his image of 'an eye sitting in a glass of water'. As he watched, the eyeball split into two, to reveal inside it a metal sphere with tiny people moving around it. As was usual with his hypnagogic visualizations, he reported that 'you can zoom in on any detail you want to see more clearly'.

The operation of at least two sub-systems becomes clearly apparent when hypnagogic subjects are asked to differentiate such imagery from dreams. They will frequently report that they are able to have other thoughts at the time, thoughts to which the images themselves seem strangely irrelevant. Some imagers are perfectly capable of carrying on a conversation while the imagery process continues. The first regular hypnagogic imager whom I studied in detail with the aid of a sound-recorder was able to inject into his hypnagogic imagery 'ordinary images'; the hypnagogic sequence continued and the ordinary images did not blend with it. A distinction seems necessary between the subject, as observing ego, and this product from his dissociated processes which we label his hypnagogic imagery. The observer sub-system is co-consciously present to note, with interest or alarm, the autonomous processes of the hypnagogic sub-system. Other emotions may accompany this observation, as we have seen (amusement, for example), and without the amnesic barrier that so often complicates the study of dreams. In waking life, as Hilgard (1977) puts it, 'the unity of consciousness is illusory'. He takes as illustration the person who listens to and comprehends another person speaking to him, while simultaneously planning his own reply. In hypnagogic imaging, as in atypical lucid dreams, this awareness of component sub-systems is even more marked.

The phenomenon of perseveration has been noted in connection with hypnagogic experiences. Perseveration of the events of the day may likewise figure prominently in dreams. The images or thoughts of the day continue without any semblance of voluntary control, and sometimes despite positive effort to stop them. Insomnia, too, may be accompanied by bouts of perseveration. On occasion this seems to involve a spontaneous emission of images and thoughts from areas of the personality not ordinarily available to consciousness. With or without the aid of hypnagogic or dream imagery, an inspiration may emerge quite spontaneously from within. A new environment, which itself often seems to stimulate hypnagogic imaging and dream recall, may provide the stimulus. External perceptual sources traditionally include the moon or a beautiful sunset; in Wordsworth's case it was the early morning view from Westminster Bridge. While in my own case no such poetic inspiration occurred, I remain indebted to an American psychologist colleague who once advised me to 'go and see the Grand Canyon, preferably from the North rim . . . it will do something to your imagery.' He was right!

It seems appropriate at this point to state that there is every

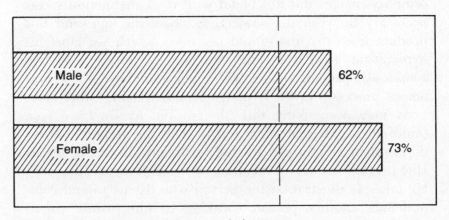

Sex difference in reporting hypnagogic imagery.

reason to regard visual, auditory and other hypnagogic imaging as normal. It is exceedingly common, and appears to be wholly compatible with good mental health. In one investiga-

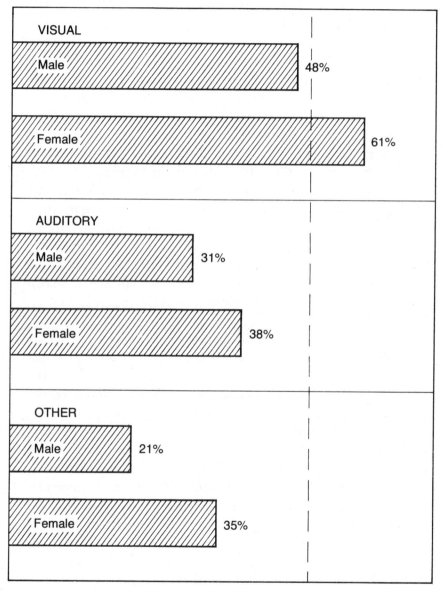

Incidence of hypnagogic imagery (n of 400).

tion of a group of Aberdeen university students we found that 64 per cent reported imagery of some kind (McKellar and Simpson 1954). My most recent findings relate to a group of 400 New Zealand university students in 1974. A clear sex difference emerged, with imagery reported by 73 per cent of the women but only 62 per cent of the men. The question then arose, which was the commoner, the visual or the auditory? The 1974 study revealed the visual kind in 61 per cent of the women and the auditory kind in only 38 per cent. Among the men, the visual was reported by 48 per cent and the auditory by 31 per cent. The sex difference remained. 'Other' kinds of hypnagogic imagery were reported by 35 per cent of women and 21 per cent of males. A typical auditory hypnagogic image often involved music or voices. Like the visual kind it was characteristically autonomous. One such imager reported: 'I lie and listen to them, and I don't know what is going to happen next.' Confusions with reality were often a feature of the auditory type of imagery. The subject would often get up with the intention of dealing with the imaged sound, as though it were a reality. In this again we see evidence that the image is 'experienced' rather than 'thought up'.

If we choose to maintain the distinction between hypnagogic imagery during the falling asleep period, and 'hypnopompic' imagery, which is a carry-over of dreamlife processes into the waking-up period, we find many instances there too of confusions with reality. (One of my favourites involves the wife of a medical practitioner who awoke to smell toast burning: 'I arose to check whether I had left the oven on, but I had not.') If this distinction is maintained it is important not to make it merely in terms of 'morning versus evening'. Clearly in the morning one can doze off again, and while drowsy have a hypnagogic image: similarly one may awake at some time other than the morning, and experience a carry-over of dreamlife, a hypnopompic image. On this point R.G. has made detailed study of his own images. At least in his own case he notices a difference between the hypnagogic images that occur in the evening, often loaded with the events of the day, and those of the morning. The evening ones tend to 'form themselves' as he watches, while the morning ones – clear as they are of perceptual experiences – are ones he tends to 'come upon' already formed.

Along with hypnagogic and hypnopompic imagery may be noted a number of other phenomena. Very common indeed is the hypnagogic 'falling experience'. The person has the impression of falling, and then of waking up with a start. In our early investigation at Aberdeen we found this hypnagogic experience to be reported by 75 per cent of subjects (182 students were investigated). It is possible that this phenomenon, so obviously related to muscular sensations (tension and relaxation), is a universal one. There are also hypnagogic and hypnopompic experiences of changes of the body-image. As illustration of this common happening I cite the subject who reported, 'I felt my body swelling like a balloon: I was being held together by bands of string in place of bones.' Another experience characteristic of both the falling-asleep and the waking-up state involves oddities of speech. One young woman awoke to find herself murmuring 'put the pink pyjamas in the salad'! These experiences (for want of a clinical name I have called them 'hypnopompic speech') have often been likened by investigators to the utterances of schizophrenic patients. Here once again it seems that processes from some system outside normal consciousness have seeped through. Indeed such speech often seems to be a comment on dream imagery of the kind that slips into forgetfulness at the moment of waking. Hypnopompic thoughts are sometimes expressed in overt speech. On other occasions they are merely thoughts, retained and expressed sub-vocally in the drowsy state before wakefulness. Their source in some system outside normal consciousness is plainly apparent to the person concerned.

Different words have been used by different investigators to label the eruptions of mental imagery from 'outside'. Freud referred to dream imagery as 'the royal road to the unconscious'.

Earlier Sir Francis Galton (1883) used the metaphor of 'a presence chamber in my mind where full consciousness holds court': near this is 'an antechamber . . . just beyond the full ken of consciousness'. Galton discusses the process of creative thinking in terms of these two chambers where 'one portion of the mind communicates with another, as with a different person'. He also examines mystical and visionary experience. He sees no mystery in the religious person, who has tuned his mind to holy ideas, finding such ideas travelling from the antechamber to the presence chamber of consciousness: his visions, thoughts and phrases are 'heard in the way so often described by devout men of all religions'.

Sleep and adjacent states of hypnagogic experience seem to encourage this passage of imagery. We shall look next at the allied hypnotic state, which William James thought had 'many affinities with ordinary sleep'. He even suggested that it is probable that we all go through such a state, transiently, when we fall asleep. This equation between the artificially induced hypnotic state and the natural hypnagogic one needs further investigation, not merely introspectively, but with appropriate physiological recordings. Nevertheless James makes the useful observation that the hypnotist keeps the subject suspended between waking and sleeping; left to himself the hypnotized subject is very liable to drop off to sleep. There are many interesting phenomena on the frontier between imagery experiences and hypnosis. They include hypnotically induced dreams, hypnotic hallucinations and various alterations of identity with accompanying imagery. These led William James himself to look to 'those deeper alterations of the personality known as automatism, double consciousness, or "second" personality for the true analogues of the hypnotic trance'.

8
Hypnotism and Hypnosis

An artificially induced state, usually (though not always) resembling sleep, but physiologically distinct from it, which is characterized by heightened suggestibility.

H. C. Warren

The terms 'hypnosis' and 'hypnotism' were introduced in 1842 by James Braid. In spite of the earlier name, 'mesmerism', and in spite of the title of his book – *The Discovery of Animal Magnetism* – Anton Mesmer certainly did not invent the art. The ancient Egyptians, Persians and Greeks all appear to have been familiar with the techniques.

A century earlier than Mesmer there lived a country gentleman named Valentine Greatrakes, who treated a variety of ailments (many, no doubt, of hysterical origin) with his 'stroking cure'. Greatrakes was a man of independent means who was rarely paid for his efforts, and it is recorded that he cured sceptics as well as believers. He conducted his 'surgery' three days a week, and among the ailments he cured were blindness and paralysis. One stout seaman, sent to him on crutches, 'walked lustily to and fro' after the stroking treatment and later claimed that he could walk ten miles. In England, as in several places on the Continent, there was a long tradition of 'royal healing'. Attitudes varied: Elizabeth I, for example, was not greatly convinced, unlike James I, who rather went in for the supernatural. Both Charles I and Charles II (who treated as many as five hundred people a year) maintained the tradition, and it was in the absence of a monarch during the Cromwellian period that Greatrakes was so much in demand. Some of his claims were put to the test. When he had 'anaesthetized' the hand of one particular patient, a pin was thrust deep into the flesh. The man declared that he had felt nothing. Greatrakes stroked the fingers a second time, the pin was again thrust in and this time the man cried out.

Anaesthesia has become a common feature of hypnotic demonstrations and experiments. In 1890 William James expressed the view that during anaesthesia 'sensitivity in the anaesthetic parts is there in the form of a secondary conscious-ness . . . susceptible to being tapped'. Hypnotically induced anaesthesias and those which occur spontaneously in hysteri-cal neurosis appear to resemble each other closely; indeed, many features of hypnosis and hysteria bear a marked resemblance.

It is difficult to discuss hypnosis in any detail without refer-ence to human suggestibility. The psychologist Cantril defines the process of suggestion as 'the acceptance of a frame of reference without intervention of the critical thought proces-ses'. Some psychologists have distinguished different kinds of suggestibility. Eysenck, for example, distinguishes a 'primary suggestibility' involving motor activity from the 'sec-ondary suggestibility' involved in anaesthesias and in positive and negative hypnotically induced hallucinations. There is good evidence to support the view that neither 'suggestibility' nor 'hypnotizability' is a unitary trait.

The scientific study of hypnosis has grown more sophisti-cated over the years. This development has been well summar-ized by Roland Shor (1972). First came Anton Mesmer (1734–1815), with his theory of 'animal magnetism'; next, the work of the Marquis of Puysegur (1751–1825), with his con-cept of an artificial somnambulism induced by responses to the wishes of the hypnotist. Then came what Shor calls the 'early psychological period', embracing on the one hand the work of Braid and on the other the work in France at Nancy of Liebault and Bernheim: the emphasis was now on the process of sugges-tion and on the suggestibility of the hypnotic subject. This was followed by the 'later psychological period', when Charcot began his work in Paris in 1878. As we have seen, two notable pupils followed Charcot's interest in hysterical neurosis and hypnotism: Sigmund Freud and Pierre Janet. Initially Freud made use of hypnotism, but he was later to abandon it in favour of his free-associative methods of therapy; as a result, psychoanalysis has been relatively indifferent to hypnotic therapy and research. In the 'early psychological period' there had been widespread use of hypnotic methods to control pain during surgical operations; Esdaile, working in India, published a substantial account of such surgery in 1850, and John Elliotson at University College Hospital, London, conducted similar operations. With the development of general anaesthetics, however, and given the influence of the psychoanalytic tradition, hypnotic methods fell out of favour.

The modern period has seen a revival of interest and some important experimental research in this area. Major investigators have included Clark Hull, Orne, Shor himself, Barber and Hilgard. Special mention must be made of the enormous amount of research conducted by T. X. Barber and his associates. Barber stands firmly in the ranks of the tough-minded. He is exceedingly critical both of clinical studies and of many previous experiments. Consider for example the 'human plank' demonstration in which a hypnotized person, under suggestion of bodily rigidity, is placed between two chairs, back of head on one, back of feet on the other. Barber presents evidence that at least 80 per cent of non-hypnotized subjects can perform this feat given suggestions of bodily rigidity. He is similarly critical of alleged age-regressions in hypnosis, hypnotic dreams, hypnotically induced hallucinations and hypnotically induced anaesthesias.

Barber's general analysis of the hypnotic situation concentrates on two things: consequent behaviour and the antecedent variables. What must be studied in consequent hypnotic behaviour are the responses to suggestion, the reports of being hypnotized, and hypnotic appearance. What must be studied amongst the antecedent variables are, first, the subject variables – embracing such things as the attitudes, expectations, and motivations of the subject – and, second, the instructive-suggestion variables – including the wording and tone of instructions, direct suggestions given, and the questions of the subsequent inquiry. None of these things is simple and all contribute to the complexity of the phenomena of hypnosis.

The mental state of the subject may be greatly altered by the suggestions given to him by the hypnotist (I have observed with interest how in one demonstration the subject became 'drunk' from a cup of pure water which he had been told was 'strong alcohol'). He may also perform some impressive imper-sonations. William James refers to the striking changes of identity which play a prominent part in public hypnotic per-formances. A subject may change himself, under the sugges-tions given, into a baby, a young lady dressing for a party, or Napoleon, or some animal. James comments on the excellence of such performances, and is not impressed with the idea that such performances can be explained away in terms of 'sham-ming or (as some modern theorists would call it) 'role playing'.

In 1939 Milton Erikson did some ingenious experiments in relation to changes of identity. In one such experiment the hypnotized subject, 'Mr Blank', was told that on waking he would no longer be 'Mr Blank'; instead he would now be 'Dr D.'. To complicate things, the real 'Dr D.', who was present, would become 'Mr Blank'. This trans-identification was remarkably effective. When wakened, the subject was ques-tioned by the pseudo 'Mr Blank' (the real Dr D.), as though he were Dr D. The subject gave an excellent account of himself (a chance conversation he had had with Dr D. provided him with a great deal of usable information: he adopted Dr D.'s manner-isms of smoking, his attitudes and his way of speaking). Asked about 'his wife', he responded naturally; asked about children, he replied with embarrassment – 'not yet'. It was only with some difficulty that the subject was re-hypnotized and restored to his true identity. In this he displayed the same resistance to being hypnotized that the real Dr D. would have shown.

That part of the scientific world which does pay attention to hypnosis is itself divided. Sutcliffe in 1960 proposed the labels 'credulous' and 'sceptical' for the two opposing camps. The credulous researchers assert the reality of hypnotic phenomena, and stress certain differences between them and phenomena which can be produced by other means. By contrast the sceptical researchers argue that the subject agrees with the hypnotist's suggestions, and acts as if they were true. Among major investigators, Hilgard, and McDougall before him, would fall into the credulous group. A leading sceptic is T. X. Barber, who contends that hypnotic phenomena can readily be produced without hypnosis. A well-known theory, influential in the early 1940s, helps to illustrate the sceptical standpoint. R. W. White held that the hypnotized subject is basically concerned to play a role – the role of the hypnotized person, as this is defined to him by the hypnotist. He is trying to behave as a hypnotized person should behave, as he understands it: his behaviour is basically goal-directed. This role-playing theory merits cautious examination. It may be agreed that, with great effort, it is possible to produce many hypnotic effects by other means, if one really wishes to. But there seem to be some thousands of years of evidence to justify regarding hypnosis as a somewhat different altered mental state. Science evaluates similarities and differences. While there are some obvious resemblances between ordinary role-playing and hypnotic behaviour, there are differences. These seem important and in the interim the hypnotic state seems to have features of its own meriting continued research. In other words I can see little merit in a 'credulous' – perhaps gullible – attitude towards the so-called 'sceptical' standpoint. And more specifically from Hilgard's important researches, as from other evidence to be cited below, the relations between hypnosis and dissociation merit re-examination.

One of the most important questions worth pursuing is this relationship between hypnosis and dissociation. Research problems in this area remain formidable. Roland Shor (1973) has analysed some of the difficulties facing the scientific investigator of hypnosis – being thought 'credulous' by his scientific colleagues is the least of his problems. Shor argues that there is a basic conflict in the scientific investigator between the tasks of hypnotist and scientist. As scientific experimenter he must maintain impartiality regarding the outcome of his research. As hypnotist he needs to maintain enthusiasm, optimism and a sense of conviction in order to produce the phenomena in the first place. Illustration may be taken from experimental attempts made to produce criminal behaviour by hypnosis in otherwise law-abiding subjects. Can this be achieved? Some investigators have claimed 'yes', others 'no'. The former have been able to argue that no amount of failures can invalidate one positive result: those who fail – excellent (sceptical) scientists though they may be – are simply incompetent hypnotists.

Taking full account both of the two camps to which Sutcliffe refers and of Shor's analysis of the problems, there is strong reason to believe that the limitations of hypnosis have been overstated. Can a person be hypnotized against his will? Can he be hypnotized when he doesn't *know* he is being hypnotized? Even as a relatively indifferent hypnotist, from my own experiments I would say 'yes'; and I have been witness to someone else's experiment in which someone standing behind the man being hypnotized was also hypnotized – *unknown even to the hypnotist*. Other questions remain: can criminal actions be induced by hypnosis? and self-destructive actions? Here too there are investigators ready to reply with an unqualified 'yes'.

The striking experiments of L. W. Rowland in the late 1930s are worth examining. In one, Rowland persuaded his subjects to make vigorous and persistent attempts to reach into a box containing a lively rattlesnake (there was a protective sheet of glass inside the box). One subject woke up when he saw the snake; but two of the others were quite happy to follow instructions, and one of them even tried to see if he could get behind the glass. Rowland's other major experiment explored the possibility of producing maliciously destructive behaviour under hypnosis. Before the experiment he demonstrated the corrosive effects of strong sulphuric acid on a strip of zinc. He then induced his subjects hypnotically to throw the acid in his face (here again, unknown to the subjects, there was a sheet of protective glass). Both subjects did, although one showed some reluctance to do so.

The power of experimenters to induce *non*-hypnotized subjects, under the influence of authoritative commands, to perform anti-social acts has been much studied in recent years. Best known are the experiments of Stanley Milgram. Milgram induced his non-hypnotized subjects to administer increasingly severe electric shocks to a victim. Deception was used: no shocks were in fact administered, but the 'victim' acted as though receiving them. The subjects giving the shocks protested; they were clearly very upset by the commands; but many of them obeyed under the influence of authority. Of forty subjects, twenty-six were prepared to continue right up to the top of the scale of intensity. These experiments have a bearing on Rowland's findings. Nevertheless I find the Rowland experiments convincing. They should certainly be kept in mind when people argue optimistically about the limited power of the hypnotist over his subject.

As regards other kinds of anti-social behaviour, experiments by W. R. Wells demonstrate that theft can be induced hypnotically. Some other experimenters in this area have had negative results – to which Wells himself responds with the argument 'failures are only failures'. Numerous failures do not invalidate a single success. Those who succeed, succeed. Failures may occur either because conditions are not optimal, or perhaps because the hypnotist himself lacks competence. My own view is that for certain hypnotic effects to be produced conditions need to be optimal. Some subjects are readily hypnotizable to a marked degree. Others have to be trained, or 'programmed' in ways analogous to a modern computer, before they can be hypnotized to produce some of the more extreme hypnotic events. Hypnotists themselves vary in their skill. The great pioneer of the school at Nancy, the rival to Charcot's Paris school, was Liebault. He claimed to be able to hypnotize over

90 per cent of all comers. His associate, Bernheim, declared that those who have not learned to hypnotize at least 80 per cent have not yet learned the skills. Some hypnotic researchers I know have claimed to be successful in the end with 100 per cent of all comers. But, as I have said, this does not necessarily mean that they have hypnotized them sufficiently deeply to produce such phenomena as hallucination and hypnotic somnambulisms. Here it would seem that further training is required.

In the literature one rather unpleasant experiment is reported in which an apparently tiresome sceptic who 'did not believe in hypnotism' was eventually hypnotized. In the hypnotic state his hands were clasped together. He was told he would not be able to unclasp them until the hypnotist permitted him. Then a lighted taper was placed between the hands, and it burned down slowly. He was not permitted to unclasp until a painful burn had occurred. Presumably this convinced him of the reality of the phenomenon. We did not like to repeat such an experiment in full, but I admit to being party, years ago, to a near-repetition. The subject held the taper between his clasped hands, release being permitted before the flame reached the hands. I observed no indication that he would have been able to unclasp them without the hypnotist's permission to do so. Under optimal conditions, the power of the hypnotist in such areas can be considerable.

There is a more positive side to the matter of hypnotic response to pain, which argues against mere role-playing theories. I refer to major operations conducted in the altered mental state, and hypnotic insensitivity to pain. Courmelles (1891), writing in the period when such operations were common, cites French data. They included amputations of the arm, of the leg and of the thigh. As we have noted, Elliotson and many others in England did similar operations. As regards hypnotizability, Hilgard (1975) estimates that 10–20 per cent of people are capable of a state of hypnosis deep enough to permit complete anaesthesia, and thus surgical operations without anaesthetics. Hilgard's own recent experimental work (which favours a dissociationist view of hypnotic anaesthesia) is impressive. In these experiments he found strong evidence that one part of the personality reported no pain, while another – a co-conscious 'hidden observer' – through automatic writing reported and assessed pain strength. (These experiments will be discussed more fully below.)

Another important aspect to consider is post-hypnotic suggestion, which played a part in the changed identity experiment involving 'Mr Blank'. In such demonstrations the subject is given instructions, while hypnotized, that on waking he will perform a specified act when a specific signal is given. In one such experiment, in which I took part, the subject was required to go to the piano and play the national anthem when the experimenter took his handkerchief out of his pocket. The instruction was faithfully obeyed, although the subject was amnesic for the fact that he had been given the suggestion. There is something most curious in the way in which the subject, in the interval which precedes the act, will ignore the task until the appropriate signal is given. As William James puts it, the suggestions 'will surge up at the pre-appointed time'. James himself regards post-hypnotic suggestion as involving experimental production of those 'second' states of the personality. He states his conviction that the consciousness which retains and holds the instruction 'is split off, dissociated from the rest of the subject's mind'. In this connection he refers to experimenters who have sought to 'tap' this 'second-state' consciousness by use of the *planchette* of the spiritualists. Gurney, for example, found evidence that people who were both good hypnotic subjects and spontaneous automatic writers would reveal through the planchette their knowledge of the post-hypnotic suggestion. This information could be tapped in the mysterious intervening period before execution of the act, despite the amnesia.

Many investigators have used hypnosis to 'tap' material not available to ordinary consciousness. William McDougall used hypnotism during World War I to treat the war-neurosis casualties of trench warfare. The hysteric, rather than organic, basis of amnesia, blindness and deafness could be diagnosed hypnotically, after which these signs and symptoms could be removed, often by post-hypnotic suggestion. More recently Wolberg (Arieti 1975) has drawn attention to the fact that a hysterical patient may develop spontaneous trance states in hypnotic sessions. There may occur fugues in which one aspect of the personality takes over and engages in unusual or anti-social behaviour, for which there later is amnesia. As Wolberg puts it, one may 'activate parts of the self that have been dissociated from the personality mainstream'.

By contrast there are many cases in which the artificially created fugue state reveals a self which is more 'normal' than the usual personality. Janet himself in 1907 presented the case of Marceline. The patient entered hospital 'in a lamentable state'. Today we might classify her as a case of 'anorexia nervosa': she was wholly unable to eat, in a state of emaciation, and if forced to eat would vomit. In addition, her vision and hearing were very bad, she was insensitive over huge areas of her skin, and she was incapable of spontaneous urination. Janet records she 'seemed to have but a breath of life left'. He treated her hypnotically. The hypnotized personality accepted food readily, and vision, hearing and skin sensitivity were normal. By a series of hypnotic treatments she was nourished and began to gain strength. She was amnesic for the hypnotic periods, and when awakened returned to her pathetic 'normal' self: inert, apathetic, semi-blind and unable to urinate. One day her parents, finding her in the hypnotized state, thought her cured and took her home. When hypnosis wore off she returned to her state of 'depression and stupefaction'. She was brought back to Pierre Janet, who decided 'to bring her back to her artificial state'. The case was under his treatment for some fifteen years. During this period Marceline would come to him to be 'put to sleep' and returned to her alert, secondary personality. (The patient eventually died of a tubercular infection.)

Another such case is known to me, which had a happier outcome. The patient came to a psychiatrist of my acquaintance (who remains anonymous) with a well-marked hysterical deafness. When hypnotized her hearing was normal. On one occasion the psychiatrist made the error of sending her home hypnotized. Then he began to think: the hypnotized personality is far better able to face life than the 'normal' personality. He proceeded to replace the one by the other. After some time he discussed with his patient the fact that he was not really necessary to the process; he instructed her in auto-hypnosis, in being able to bring back her hearing by putting herself into the hypnotic personality. She took up a part-time post which left her the full morning to work herself into the state of being able to hear. In effect the treatment amounted to replacing the disturbed primary personality with the healthier, albeit hypnotized, secondary personality. The cure was effective.

Very frequently a hypnotic session involves a demonstration of hallucination, positive or negative. In positive hallucination the individual 'perceives' something which is not there. In negative hallucination there is a failure to perceive some aspect of the environment which is present. To illustrate, in one of Erikson's experiments a persistent buzzer was used to help induce the hypnotic state. The two subjects used were given, under hypnosis, the suggestion that they had become deaf. For a time, response to the buzzer ceased to be reported, but it returned when the hypnotic deafness was removed. Quite often the subject is given the false suggestion that somebody has left the room. He responds by treating this person as no longer present. Such happenings are a familiar feature of many public hypnotic demonstrations. William James discusses similar evidence. If a stroke is made on a piece of paper and the subject is hypnotically required to 'not perceive' it, he will do so. While the subject is not looking, the original stroke is then surrounded by other, similar strokes. The subject will point out, one by one, the new strokes, but continue to ignore the original one. He remains capable of distinguishing, with great accuracy, the original stroke from all the others, as they are added to the paper. In some way or other he has to perceive, and discriminate, in order to know which to not-perceive.

These paradoxical forms of behaviour have been the subject of some interesting experimental studies in the field of negative hallucination. Such work will be discussed with particular reference to McDougall's 'Five Stamps' experiment, which has impressed me as one of the most interesting, and thought-provoking, in the whole research literature of psychology.

9
Hypnosis and the 'Five Stamps' Experiment

*The paradox that the stamps are seen, and yet not seen . . .
can only be resolved by the hypothesis that he at the time is a
divided personality, one part of which sees the two stamps
and prevents the other part from seeing them.*

William McDougall

Negative hallucination may be illustrated from some experiments with nitrous oxide conducted by Steinberg in 1956. In
one such experiment the subject reported that the table at
which he was sitting disappeared, and 'only the pencil and
paper remained "suspended in mid air" '. Later he reported of
someone standing in the room that 'only a pair of legs
remained, the upper part of the body had disappeared, and the
wall was visible behind'. On the whole negative hallucinations
are rarely reported outside hypnosis. In hypnosis, under the
influence of suggestion, the subject frequently fails to perceive
some person or object actually present in the room. We have
noted, however, that the subject seems to perceive in some way
in order not to perceive.

In 1962 Martin Orne studied this paradoxical behaviour by
comparing hypnotized subjects with others who were asked to
act as though hypnotized. Their behaviour was markedly different. The subjects were 'given' a negative hallucination of a
chair. When asked to walk about the room, those who had not
in fact been hypnotized would bump into the chair: the reason
they gave was that they were supposed not to see it, and that
walking around it would show that they had seen it. The
hypnotized subjects, on the other hand, would actively avoid
the chair, and they would afterwards report 'not having seen

McDOUGALL'S FIVE STAMPS EXPERIMENT

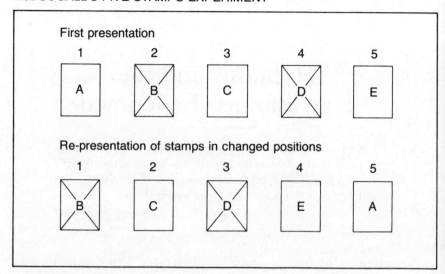

First presentation

1   2   3   4   5

A   B   C   D   E

Re-presentation of stamps in changed positions

1   2   3   4   5

B   C   D   E   A

the chair . . . but having seen an empty space'. This space was described by one of the hypnotic subjects as 'somewhat more empty than the rest of empty space'. Orne concluded from these experiments that his hypnotized subjects were in some way or other able to perceive and not perceive the chair at the same time: 'at some level they are aware of the chair.' Such experiments lead us into a fascinating area of paradoxes. The story begins in 1926 when William McDougall reported his 'Five Stamps' experiment.

McDougall placed five unused postage stamps of the same design in front of the hypnotized subject. He then pointed to two of the stamps and indicated that they would no longer be there when the subject looked again. Asked to point out the stamps he now saw, the subject ignored the two taboo stamps and pointed out the remaining three. Out of sight, McDougall then changed the positions of the stamps and asked him to count them out again. *Which two stamps did the subject now no longer see?* Did he respond merely positionally – that is, ignore the two stamps which now occupied the positions of the tabooed stamps? Or did he respond to the objects themselves – that is, continue to ignore the same two stamps despite their new positions? McDougall reports a continued failure to perceive the same two stamps. This could only mean that the tabooed stamps were not merely perceived in some way, but were also discriminated from the others. If not perceived how could they be singled out for neglect? After the experiment, when the subject was awakened from hypnosis, he still negatively hallucinated the same two stamps. McDougall restored their visibility by taking the subject's finger and touching the edge of first one stamp, then the other. The stamps became visible, at first dimly and later in full colour and form. McDougall interprets his experiment in terms of dissociation. He argues that we can no longer speak of the subject as 'B', an integrated personality, but rather as 'B1 and B2, B's two separately functioning parts'.

Thirty years later Henry Tonn and I repeated this experiment (1967). We introduced some variations, because we were interested in both negative and positive hallucination. Our subjects were two male American university students aged twenty years and of above average intelligence. The materials we used were five unused American postage stamps in current use, carrying the face of George Washington. For brevity I will speak of a 'positional response' as response to the positions only, and an 'object response' as response to the particular stamps despite their new positions. We were not interested in how people behave in hypnosis generally, but simply to see if it was possible to replicate McDougall's experiment. This involved setting up two different perceptual systems in the same subject, one of which perceived and the other of which failed to perceive. With the first subject we failed on a direct repetition of McDougall's experiment. The subject responded to the positions only, and saw the two taboo stamps in their new positions. We attempted a number of other presentations with objects which were easier to distinguish; these included cigarette cartons of different designs, chess pieces and coins. In the case of the coins – standard American 1-cent pieces – the two taboo ones were bright and shining and looked markedly different from the others. With these objects we were successful in establishing negative hallucination.

The main interest of our first experiment was the post-hypnotic period: on return to normality, the subject still had great difficulty in seeing the taboo coins. We picked up the coins and dropped them – the subject heard the noise but still did not see them. We moved the coins about and the subject spontaneously remarked: 'do you enjoy moving empty spaces around?' We put the subject's finger on one of the stamps, but for him – unlike McDougall's subject – even this was not sufficient. He remarked: 'something's adhering but there's nothing there . . . that's an empty space.' Only finally, and with some effort, were we able to restore vision. The subject exhibited surprise as 'it gradually came into view, blurry at first but quite clearly after about a second'. We did not obtain introspections from the subject because we had given him the suggestion of post-hypnotic amnesia.

In a second experiment, with another subject, we decided to build up a learning set progressing from easier to more difficult acts of discrimination. This subject was carefully instructed to remember everything that happened to him.

First Presentation
Five chessmen were used, two bishops and three other pieces. Negative hallucination was given for the two bishops. An object response followed their re-presentation in different positions. The subject continued to not-see the two bishops. Negative hallucination persisted.

Second Presentation
Five Amercian 1-cent coins were used. Three were dull, the other two were bright and shining and readily distinguishable. Given re-presentation of these two, the subject again gave object responses to them – i.e., failed to see them in their new positions. Again negative hallucination.

Third Presentation

Training proceeded with five playing cards, three black and two tabooed red cards. A positive, object response, again followed.

Fourth Presentation

For this we returned to postage stamps. These were again George Washington 5-cent stamps. We made differentiation easy by leaving margin paper at the top of the two taboo stamps. Again there was a positive, object response.

Fifth Presentation

This was a return to the original McDougall experiment. We removed the identifying margin paper, presented the stamps, tabooed two, and then sought response to their re-presentation in different positions. The results were negative. The subject responded positionally only.

Sixth Presentation

At this stage we decided to introduce a modification of the procedure and bring in positive as well as negative hallucination. The playing cards were used again. The two red taboo cards were first tabooed at positions 1 and 2, there being no cards at positions 3, 4 and 5. Asked to point out the cards he 'saw', the subject pointed to positions 3, 4 and 5. In other words he pointed to three non-existent cards as the ones he 'saw'. He named these cards 'correctly' with the names of the three black cards he had already seen. He ignored the two taboo cards actually present. This presentation was repeated, with the same result.

Seventh Presentation

We started with five coins, tabooing the two bright, easily discriminated ones. We then added below another row of five more coins, and then a third. Object results continued to occur. At first three coins were seen, then eight, then thirteen. The taboo coins continued not to be 'seen', despite the addition of new coins that had not been used before. The purpose of this demonstration was to show to our satisfaction that the taboo coins really were 'seen' in order to be 'not-seen'. He did not, and could not, discriminate simply by recognizing the remaining (now new) coins. After this training we returned to the five stamps.

Eighth Presentation

This was the crucial part of the experiment. The subject was presented with five postage stamps with no obvious basis (other than minor differences of perforation) for discriminating between them. We asked him to look very carefully at all five of them. The stamps in positions 3 and 5 were tabooed. Then, while the subject's vision was prevented, we replaced the taboo stamps in positions 1 and 4. *What now occurred was an object response:* the subject on re-presentation pointed to positions 2, 3 and 5, ignoring the taboo stamps in their new positions 1 and 4. We had replicated McDougall's experiment, although in our case only after a period of training in discrimination. Immediately afterwards we repeated the presentation, although this

EIGHTH PRESENTATION

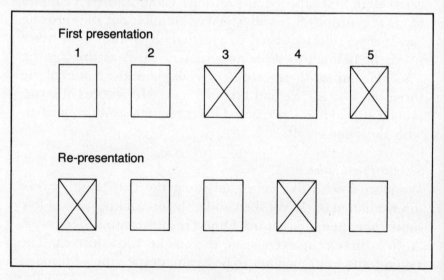

time with an only partially positive response. The subject responded positionally to one of the stamps on its re-presentation, and gave object response to the other. A further presentation yielded a wholly negative (purely positional) response. But on yet another presentation we obtained a wholly positive response.

Ninth Presentation

The subject's positive response was now studied in detail. This involved performance of some extremely difficult tasks. (It may be stressed that presentation eight and all subsequent presentations were made with the 'difficult' stamps; the same five stamps were used, and different stamps were tabooed on different occasions.) We proceeded to add positive to negative hallucination:

1. Taboo stamps in positions 1 and 5. Other stamps in positions 2, 3 and 4. The three non-taboo stamps were all removed, and the subject asked to point out the stamps he now 'saw'. He pointed to the three blank spaces, ignoring the actual stamps at 1 and 5.

2. Taboo stamps at 1 and 5. On re-presentation a taboo stamp was left at position 1, and a non-taboo stamp put at position 5. There were blank spaces at 2, 3 and 4. The subject 'saw' the stamp at position 5 (previously occupied by a taboo stamp) and the vacant spaces at positions 2, 3 and 4, and ignored the taboo stamp at position 1.

3. Taboo stamps at 1 (again) and 3, and a third stamp at position 5. As what he 'saw' the subject pointed to 2, 4 and 5.

4. On this occasion the stamps were tabooed at 1 and 5, and re-presented at 4 and 5, a non-taboo stamp being put in position 1. Subject pointed to the stamp at position 1, then the blank spaces at 2 and 3, ignoring the taboo stamps at 4 and 5.

The subject's external responses throughout our experiment were fascinating. He showed his ability to hallucinate 'correctly', that is in accord with instructions, both positively and negatively. He followed the complex interchangings of the stimulus objects (three types of response were occurring: first, stamps visible to the experimenters were also visible to the subject; then, stamps not visible to the experimenters were 'seen' by the subject; then, stamps visible to the experimenters were 'not-seen' by the subject). His ability to discriminate was quite remarkable.

The subject's subjective experience and introspective report were clearly going to be of enormous interest. These introspections were obtained from him after he had been wakened from hypnosis. They gave clear evidence that he had not seen the taboo stamps during the hypnotic period, with one interesting exception. This was during the eighth presentation when he gave a 'mixed' response. Of this he said, 'It didn't seem to be right.' He added 'there was a stamp in my mind but there wasn't . . . it seemed like a stamp wasn't there but it was there . . . you took it away but it was still there . . . the rest was clear after that . . . you took them away and they weren't there.' It may be added that on no occasion were the taboo stamps actually removed, the 'took them away' response was purely a response to the taboo. The earlier (training) part of the experiment had produced similar negative hallucination. For example (presentation three) he was able to name the cards correctly: 'You told me the diamonds were gone and I would see the spades – you took them away.' Of the coins he said, 'Where the shiny ones had been there were just spaces.' Regarding their re-presentation he said, 'The spaces were not filled, but there were other spaces.' These other 'spaces' were the ones now occupied by the taboo coins. The introspections obtained accord closely with what would be expected from the behavioural performance. The subjective accompaniment to the suggestion to hallucinate negatively was either 'a blank space' or 'you had taken them away'.

In his discussion of his original experiment, McDougall wrote that 'any normal person can, by close inspection, discriminate and recognize one or two postage stamps among others.' This was certainly what was happening in our experiment with the hypnotized subject. With reference to the stamps, the subject remarked spontaneously that we had 'taken different ones away' – that is tabooed different stamps – on different occasions. This accorded with our actual procedure. The stamps used would have been familiar to the subject throughout the experiment. To prepare the 'difficult stamps' task we removed the margin paper from the original two taboo stamps; they and other stamps in the set of five were then tabooed in different presentations, with no basis of discrimination other than slight variations of perforation. The subject explained that he had recognized individual stamps from the way they had been torn from the sheet: one stamp had 'a round corner', another 'a knob' and a third 'a square bottom'. McDougall claimed that 'any normal person' (i.e., a person not hypnotized) can perform similar feats. We had conducted our own experiment at New Mexico Highlands University. Following my return to Britain, Henry Tonn agreed to conduct a control experiment to investigate McDougall's claim.

In our control experiment, the subjects were non-hypnotized people and the materials were 'difficult' stamps similar in design to those we had used in the hypnotic experiments. They were not the same five stamps. Frankly I was not prepared to part with them, or risk them in the post. This weakness must be admitted. But, as in the original experiment the 5-cent stamps (again George Washington design) required very close inspection for them to be distinguished. There were five male students aged nineteen or twenty, and one female aged eighteen. All were required, unhypnotized, to inspect the stamps closely. The procedure of the main experiment then followed. Subjects were required to point to the 'blank spaces' occupied by the taboo stamps. In only two of twenty-three complex re-presentations were the correct stamps distinguished. Both these correct choices were followed by failures, suggesting that they were lucky guesses.

The introspections of the control subjects were interesting. One subject refused to believe that the stamps could be differentiated from one another, and simply didn't try. Another accurately differentiated the stamps but got hopelessly confused when their positions were changed. Four subjects remarked that they probably could have distinguished between the stamps, but were unable to summon up the motivational effort to do this. This remark resembles a comment made by the hypnotic subject who had put up such remarkable performances in our original second experiment. He said that he wished that he could pursue his studies with as much concentrative power as he had been able to use when hypnotized in distinguishing the five stamps.

The results of our study, like those of McDougall's original experiment, support a dissociationist view of the hypnotic state. It may be stressed again that we were not concerned with how people in general perform when hypnotized. Individual differences in hypnotizability are well established, and have been intensively studied. Our interest was to verify whether a subject could be hypnotized in sufficient depth to replicate the original experiment. In other words: is it possible to set up, in the same person, two different perceptual sub-systems? This we were able to do, but only after a period of training. In our case, as in McDougall's, it was necessary for one such subsystem to 'see' and discriminate, so that the other system could discriminate and 'not-see'. Perceptual system S1 perceived; perceptual system S2 did not perceive. The additional positive-negative hallucination procedures support this dissociationist interpretation. Some of the other features of the experiment, in relation to both method and interpretation, are discussed elsewhere (McKellar and Tonn 1967; McKellar 1968).

McDougall's 'Five Stamps' experiment, and our repetitions of it, concerned visual perception. Some important parallel experiments involving the perception of pain have been conducted in recent years by E. R. Hilgard. In referring to the experiments and Hilgard's report of them in the *Psychological Review*, a major Canadian psychologist, Donald Hebb, assesses them as 'the most important current development in psychology, with a potential significance for the understanding of mind that is hard to estimate'. Hilgard's 'hidden observer' experiments are analogous to McDougall's five stamps, in that they involve two different perceptual systems. They also represent an experimental analogue to spontaneous instances of co-consciousness. It will be remembered that if people had taken seriously the introspections of the co-conscious Sally Beauchamp, we might have known much more about dream-life many years earlier than Kleitman. Fortunately, as Hebb's assessment indicates, the scientific world is listening to Hilgard.

In the context of surgical uses of hypnotism, Hilgard himself cites the early work of Durand de Gros in 1868, with his theory of 'multiple layers of consciousness'. Although the patient during surgery does not consciously experience pain, he nevertheless does experience pain in one of his 'sub-egos'. As is well known, in a hysteria patient anaesthesia may occur spontaneously, without hypnosis. Of such patients William James wrote that, 'sensitivity in the anaesthetic parts is also there, in the form of a secondary consciousness'. He added that this sub-system is 'susceptible to being tapped and made to testify to its existence in various odd ways' (James 1890). In 1960, Kaplan conducted an experiment which gave striking support to this view. The subject in hypnosis was given the suggestion that his left hand would be insensitive to pain and that his right hand would perform the actions of continuous automatic writing. The left hand was pricked by a needle. The right hand wrote, 'Ouch, damn it, you're hurting me.' After a few minutes the subject asked the experimenter, 'When are you going to begin?' Kaplan interpreted these paradoxical events, as did de Gros, in terms of 'sub-egos'. In some way or other the subject experienced the pain. This secondary perceptual system manifested its co-conscious existence through automatic writing.

Hilgard (1973, 1975) systematically explored this phenomenon. In one set of experiments he induced pain by immersing the hand of the hypnotized subject in iced water. The subject himself reported no pain in any direct way. But Hilgard had built into his subject a 'hidden observer'. This sub-system, split off from consciousness, reported pain, again through automatic writing. As instructed, it gave quantitative assessments of the amount of pain experienced. Again we find a close parallel to the spontaneous occurrences of hysteria in which pain is both felt and not felt. With hysterical anaesthesias, the 'say yes when you feel it, and say no when you don't feel it' test has been widely used. Any 'no' response is paradoxical, as in the Kaplan and Hilgard experiments.

In interpreting his research findings Hilgard refers to a 'split between two cognitions'. In the experiment, 'cognition A' experiences pain and reports the amount of pain through the automatic writing of the 'hidden observer', while 'cognition B' fails to experience pain. In these circumstances the hidden observer operates like an introspectively alert Sally who is co-conscious and overlooks the total situation. As we have seen, primary personalities are not always pleased to learn about the co-conscious sub-systems within them. Hilgard questioned his subjects on this matter, and reactions varied. One reported annoyance about the 'hidden observer', who was looking on in a superior fashion and amused at the subject's self-deception. Another reported a sense of satisfaction in having a kind of guardian angel there to protect his body against his own failure to process information accurately. Of interest is Hilgard's observation that the 'hidden observer' as a sub-system gave no evidence of regression, or performance at a lower level of cognitive functioning. He – or 'it' – used the same level of conceptual language as the subject, and proved fully capable of a quantitative estimate of the amount of pain experienced.

Hilgard has taken a stand on the basis of these and his many other studies of the hypnotic state. His plea for a new look at dissociation is worth attending to. He himself is highly critical both of 'role-playing' accounts of hypnosis and of comfortable beliefs about the 'limitations' of hypnotism. His subjects as hidden observers support his own view of hypnosis as a dissociative phenomenon. As one reported, 'there's Me 1, Me 2 and Me 3. Me 1 is hypnotized, Me 2 is hypnotized and observing, and Me 3 is when I'm awake' (Hilgard 1977, p. 210). The standpoint accords with James's and McDougall's views of hypnotic dissociation. Hilgard also argues that 'dissociation', or at least 'neo-dissociation', has major implications within psychology as a whole. He contends, as did Morton Prince, and as I have argued in this book, that there are many minor forms of dissociation which can help increase our understanding of the normal human personality.

10
Dissociation Revisited

Dissociation theory went out of favour without effective criticism. Other topics in psychology have had their day, suffered periods of neglect, and then returned.

E. R. Hilgard

The neglected concept of dissociation does seem to give us a fresh slant on a wide range of psychological phenomena. Investigations suggest that the idea of personality sub-systems, linked but with amnesic barriers between them, may help us make a rather more sophisticated classification of mental behaviour than has usually been the case. The mainstream of psychology has tended to neglect this approach, and its analysis as a result has exaggerated the distinctions between the normal and the abnormal.

My own interest in dissociation has arisen from a study of imagery, particularly the autonomous forms of imagery so typical of dreamlife and the hypnagogic state. The marked independence, spontaneity and originality of this imagery have seemed to me to demand dissociationist examination. That great advocate of dissociation theory, Hilgard, talks in terms of subordinate personality systems, appropriate to varying roles, which 'lose communication' with each other. In his view, these separate systems can be identified as relatively coherent patterns of behaviour, each with 'sufficient complexity to represent some degree of internal organization; an amnesic barrier commonly divides and prevents integration between these systems – although in the apparent 'possession' by an alien personality this amnesia is not always complete (as Morton Prince recognized). Most importantly, Hilgard recognizes the many minor dissociations in our everyday experience, such as automatisms and obsessive thoughts.

We have noted the growing interest of experimental psychology in what is called state dependency. Much research has been done into the effects of hallucinogens and other drugs, and the study of altered mental states generally is quite prominent. Cross-cultural psychology has also made great advances and there is increasing interest in comparisons between our own modes of thinking and those characteristic of less developed societies. As we saw, the multiple personality of the Asian girl, 'Soosan', was interpreted as 'possession' by her family, but in naturalistic terms by her psychiatrist investigator: attribution theory seeks to distinguish the cultural pressures behind such differing interpretations of subjective events.

There are sub-groups even in Western societies who are prepared to give crystal-gazing, automatic writing and lucid dreaming explanations which have little in common with naturalistic science. Classic conversion hysteria of the kind studied by Charcot, Janet and Freud may be rare in Europe today, but it is very common indeed if we are prepared to overcome our parochialism and consider other countries of the world. The decline of conventional major religions seems to have done much to encourage an 'open' attitude to the occult. This has affected the Western world to a marked degree. In the realm of major psychiatric illnesses we encounter patients who regard their 'voices' not as their own autonomous auditory imagery but as evidence of 'possession' by some alien entity. And we know very well how easily, under the influence of such factors as fatigue, sensory deprivation, drowsiness and hallucinogenic drugs, distinctions between 'mere imagery' and 'hallucination' may break down. There are many gradations of subjective experience, and in any attempt to classify them our labels, language and vocabulary limit us severely.

Under the heading of 'state dependency', experimental psychologists have developed a renewed interest in dissociative phenomena. State dependency was discussed in Chapter 2 in connection with the insights of Wilkie Collins in his novel *The Moonstone*. We saw how Collins, presumably influenced by the work of Dr Elliotson on hypnotic somnambulism, developed his plot: under the influence of laudanum a sub-system of Franklin Blake's personality takes over; in his normal state of wakefulness there is amnesia for its actions; given laudanum a second time, the secondary personality system returns. Writing of dissociation, Bernard Hart said that 'the various elements of mental machinery' seem to be 'organized into different functional systems by the throwing in of the appropriate gear' (Hart 1939). Franklin Blake's actions are explained by Collins in a similar way, in terms of the interaction of two sub-systems with an amnesic barrier between them. The experimental study of 'state dependency' has taken such problems into the laboratory: the experiments focus on the dissociative behaviour of memory systems under the influence of drugs. In my consideration of sleep, wakefulness and the adjacent hypnagogic state I have discussed very similar happenings. To suggest another analogy, dissociation can be very like tuning in first on one radio station and then on another which excludes the first: on a wide wave-band we may, as in the hypnagogic state, be able to listen to both programmes at once. The spontaneous co-consciousness of Eve Black, Sally Beauchamp and Vicky Dorsett is a rarity, but these extreme cases may be useful reference points. As the 'hidden observer' experiments have shown, Hilgard was able to produce remarkably similar phenomena experimentally in the laboratory.

An alternative to the psychoanalytic concept of the Unconscious, placing more emphasis on sub-systems and the links between them, may have advantages. It can often be observed even during psychoanalysis that therapy is less a matter of bringing to consciousness wholly forgotten memories than of establishing linkages. The memories, images and motivational systems involved may be conscious; what is important is their significance in relation to one another. Interplay between these sub-systems can be observed in patients diagnosed as schizophrenic; in the normal personality it is the linkages that are 'unconscious', rather than the actual sub-systems.

Many investigators – Yellowlees (1932) for example – conceive of hallucinations as ideas and images which intrude on the consciousness from outside. Sometimes they are benign, on other occasions they are malevolent and threatening. Morton Prince, on the other hand, regarded hallucination as an emergence into consciousness of imagery from another stream of mental life. The two streams follow parallel paths much of the time, but occasionally they cross. A process of this kind is particularly apparent in certain multiple-personality cases. Eve White came for treatment complaining of hallucinations for which Eve Black eventually accepted responsibility. In the Beauchamp case the harassed B4 actually insisted in her ultimatum that Sally stop inflicting them. In several cases one of the personalities was able to stay awake while another slept; the waking, co-conscious personality was then able to inflict its thoughts on the sleeper through dreams.

Undoubtedly there is considerable overlap between the phenomena of normal mental life – thinking, efforts to remember, voices of conscience, and imagery, for example – and those liable to be diagnosed as 'hallucination'. This is particularly the case with people diagnosed as 'psychiatric patients'. I have often found patients, even 'schizophrenics', telling me about their hypnagogic imagery, and such imagery seemed very similar to the hypnagogic imagery related to me by other people – indeed the psychotic patients often interpreted it in the same way as I did. On occasion in interviews with patients I have found that their 'voices' or the things they 'saw' occurred more frequently at night. One such patient, representative of several, told me of menacing and 'spiteful faces' which appeared to her in the hospital ward. These seem remarkably similar to the 'faces in the dark' type of hypnagogic imagery, a commonplace and normal phenomenon. On another occasion the same patient saw 'a walrus and a tiger' which came and sat on her bed. Such visual hypnagogic images occur commonly, and have often been reported to me by people I have no reason to believe are psychotic. Colleagues who specialize in clinical psychology have informed me that from time to time they have encountered talk of 'hallucination' in psychiatric case notes, when the phenomena were clearly hypnagogic images. I have encountered several people who have sought psychiatric help, believing themselves hallucinated, purely because of common-or-garden hypnagogic imagery.

It is by no means easy, indeed perhaps it is impossible, to lay down clear criteria distinguishing 'hallucination' from many related phenomena. When one encounters patients who have actually kept a diary of their hallucinations, the criterion of 'having insight' into the subjectivity of the experiences is unconvincing. There are many circumstances – sensory deprivation and hallucinogen experiments, for example – in which situational pressures will evoke 'hallucination' in most people, and occasional hallucinations seem to be fully compatible with normal mental life. In his pioneer study of imagery, Galton found strong evidence of a continuum ranging from 'imagery' to 'hallucination'. Large-scale investigations like Sidgwick's 'Census of Hallucinations' revealed that just under 10 per cent of people had experienced a 'hallucination' at some time of their lives. This study explicitly excluded hypnagogic experiences. So-called 'motoring hallucinations' are commonly reported under conditions of fatigue. As one subject told me he would 'quite often swerve to avoid people and dogs that aren't there'. Under conditions of drowsiness, and in the hypnagogic state itself, the distinction between what is and what is not a hallucination becomes blurred. Similarly, on waking up many people confuse their hypnopompic imagery with reality. As so often in psychology, criterion problems are formidable here, and our existing vocabulary sadly inadequate. Those images which exhibit a large measure of autonomy without conscious control are particularly foxing, and they figure prominently in experiences liable to be classified as hallucinatory.

A significant distinction can be made between the *molar*

dissociations of multiple personality, and the *molecular* dissociations of the schizophrenias. The personality of the schizophrenic is not 'split' into a finite number of sub-systems, it is 'shattered' into innumerable fragments. Ideas, impulses, images and emotional upsurges function without restraint. Control by a central ego system is minimal, and in the early phases a patient may have acute introspective awareness of this loss of control within him. Ideas may erupt into consciousness to be interpreted as things 'put into' the mind by some malevolent, external agency. To outside observation the individual's behaviour is chaotic and unpredictable. As a result of the confusion experienced introspectively, either the weakened ego system is overwhelmed or some attempt is made to explain these autonomous processes. The latter can lead to the development of delusions – delusions of persecution, or of influence from outside. Some patients will talk volubly about their persecutory or other delusions; by contrast others are so absorbed in the autonomous processes that they are unwilling, or unable, to communicate at all. Many patients resemble the central character 'K', in Franz Kafka's novel *The Trial*: in this nightmare story, K is buffeted by forces he cannot control, and by events he cannot understand. In *The Trial*, and again in *The Castle*, events happen without apparent cause. The central character of *The Castle* constantly finds unpredictable and inexplicable things going on behind the doors of different rooms. The doors are often closed against him, and there are discontinuities in the passage of time.

When in 1911 Eugene Bleuler coined the word 'schizophrenia', he was influenced by the work of Pierre Janet on dissociation. Bleuler himself commented on the difference between the dissociated hysteric, who had interested Janet, and the schizophrenic. In the schizophrenic psychoses the splitting is 'more lawless, worse determined . . . the schizophrenic psyche is infinitely more split than the hysteric'. We are no longer dealing with several sub-systems but with a larger number of small mental components. Karl Menninger is

among those who use the term 'fragments'. Menninger sees no
difficulty in conceiving of both hallucination and delusion in
such terms. He writes that 'groups of ideas, together with their
emotional concomitants, may become split off from the main
personality', and he suggests that their relationship is 'something like the moon and the earth'. Let us extend this analogy:
a system comprising a heavenly body and one satellite, the
earth and the moon, could represent dual personality; Mars
with its two satellites could represent the triumvirate of
Christine Beauchamp; outer planets such as Jupiter, with its
eight major satellites, could stand for more fragmented dissociations such as those of Sybil or Eve. But what of the
disintegration of the schizophrenic? Estimates of the asteroid
belt range from 40,000 to 100,000 tiny particles of matter –
these behave unpredictably, according to principles which we
have not yet understood.

There are certain resemblances between the molar and the
molecular forms of dissociation; indeed, in marginal cases it
may be difficult to decide which diagnostic label should be
used. It is my belief that if we study the Kafkaesque time
discontinuities and periodic amnesias of the multiple personality we may glimpse an understanding of some of the more
baffling features of that group of psychoses, 'the schizophrenias'. Some schizophrenic patients will name their hallucinatory voices and attribute further characteristics to them
in much the same way as do the cases of multiple personality;
and there are many lesser dissociative phenomena, quite
common in normal mental life (particularly those connected
with upsurges of imagery), which occur as much in the psychotic as in the hysteric dissociative states. I cannot begin to go
into the formidable problems of schizophrenia in any detail
here, but it does seem worth pointing out that there are some
links with the molar dissociations which I have been discussing
in this book. The relationship is undoubtedly a complex one,
but it can be instructive.

Diagnosis has its different preferences and schools of

thought their different languages. In the context of this personal choice of vocabulary amongst investigators it is well worth examining some of the early cases of Breuer and Freud. Their *Studies on Hysteria* (1893–95) is an important book. It presents four of Freud's main cases, one of Breuer's and theoretical discussions by both investigators. It was out of the study of these patients – diagnosed as hysterical neurotics – that psychoanalysis developed.

From its early period, psychoanalysis brought with it a healthy interest in the individual and a deep and persistent curiosity about what goes wrong with individual lives. On the whole Freud and Breuer emerge from the books as much less interested in the phenomena of hysteria than in evolving a suitable method of treatment. The major innovation was the cathartic, 'talking out', cure initiated by Breuer. (Freud's patient 'Elizabeth von R.' made a considerable contribution: she was resistant to hypnosis, but managed to engage in the process of catharsis in a state of full wakefulness.) Breuer's case, 'Anna O.', is most interesting. She came to Breuer in 1880, at the age of twenty-one, and one of her main presenting symptoms was hallucination. Her neurosis related to the devotion with which she had nursed her father, who had died the previous year. The case has been cited repeatedly over the years by writers in support of psychoanalysis, and as Ellenberger (1972) points out after detailed re-examination of the original case-notes it has been somewhat oversimplified. Understandably perhaps, everyone latches on to the talking out cure.

The catharsis method was developed by Freud. It became the basis of his psychoanalytic free-association method once he had abandoned the technique of hypnosis originally used by Breuer. The focus turned towards analytic therapy and away from hypnotic treatments and descriptions of the phenomena of hysteria. Writing of Freud's methods, Janet observes that 'what I referred to as psychological dissociation . . . he baptised with the name of catharsis' (cited in McDougall 1926).

Closely associated with the talking out activity was what Freud called abreaction – the reliving of a past emotional experience. Janet has much to say about this too, although he uses a different terminology. His own cases include Irénè, who in somnambulistic episodes relived the death of her mother, and a young girl called Ra, who had been ill-treated by a former employer and 'acted over and over again the scenes she had lived through'.

In his biography of Freud (1953), Ernest Jones identified Anna O. She proved to be one Bertha Pappenheim, the daughter of a well-to-do Viennese family; she was an intelligent, well-educated young woman who later wrote short stories and plays as well as being a valued and distinguished welfare worker. From the various sources we can gather quite a full picture of the case.

Breuer states that 'two entirely distinct states of consciousness were present . . . [they] alternated very frequently and without warning' (Breuer and Freud). One of these personalities was a sad, conscientious individual, the other was disturbed and agitated and subject to frightening hallucinations. The Ellenberger records reveal a fact of some interest: the secondary personality lived precisely 365 days earlier than the primary one. In other words, Anna would hallucinate events that had occurred, day for day, one year earlier. Breuer's own case-report of 1882 revealed in some detail what Anna referred to as her 'time missing'. Her time discontinuities are remarkably similar to those we have seen in multiple personality cases. She would, for example, wake up in the night, in bed, to discover that her stockings were still on; and she had no apparent memory of how this had happened. Breuer himself makes repeated references to her having 'lost' time. He quotes comments in which she would 'remark upon the gap in her train of conscious thought' (Breuer and Freud). Anna herself referred to her secondary personality as her 'bad self'. Breuer likened it to a dream, characterized by imagining and hallucinating and exhibiting large gaps of memory. On one occasion he discusses a waking dream in which Anna saw a threatening black snake approaching her father's bed. He adds that 'her hallucinatory *absences* were filled with terrifying figures, death's heads and skeletons' (Breuer and Freud).

Apart altogether from these hallucinations, Anna emerges as a person very much given to what Breuer calls 'habitual daydreaming'. This seems to have been an escape from the monotonous life she led. Anna herself spoke of her 'private theatre' (Ellenberger 1972). There are many resemblances between Anna's 'bad self' and those other secondary personalities (Sally, for instance) which we have already encountered. Breuer refers to this personality system as lazy, disagreeable and ill-natured. He adds that her 'true character' was the opposite of these. An examination of Breuer's records, as indeed of the original Breuer and Freud book alone, indicates that Breuer could easily have chosen to write of 'Anna A', and 'Anna B'. A terminology consistent with the dissociationist tradition would have been wholly appropriate to this case, and Freud's biographer says quite firmly that 'it was a case of double personality': he refers to 'two distinct states of consciousness', one of which was 'a naughty and troublesome child' (Jones 1953). While Anna was in this secondary personality, Breuer records how she would throw cushions and tear off buttons; he reports her as speaking of 'having two selves, a real one and an evil one' – the latter 'forced her to behave badly' (Breuer and Freud).

Of interest in Freud's contribution to the *Studies of Hysteria* is his defence of the use of analogies. In seeking to explain the dynamics of the patients discussed he uses a chemical analogy. He refers to a 'psychical group' that has been 'split off' and plays the part of a crystal 'from which a crystallization which would otherwise not have occurred will start with the greatest facility'. In other words, a sub-system of the personality 'crystallizes out' as does a chemical super-saturated solution that has been seeded with a crystal. It is increasingly apparent that whether or not such a patient is actually labelled a case of 'multiple personality' is little more than a choice of words. What Freud is saying is consistent with the account William James gives of the development of a secondary pesonality. It also accords closely with Dostoevksy's insights – expressed through Ivan Karamazov – into how what Freud was later to call 'repression' may contribute to the development of such multiple personality.

It was conflict within the individual – intra-psychic conflict – that divided the personality of Anna O., just as it was conflict that divided Christine Beauchamp, Eve, Mary Reynolds, May Naylor, Spanish Maria. Their various investigators simply chose different words to describe these happenings. In the literary field, where Frankenstein has his monster and Dr Jekyll his Mr Hyde, we have seen clearly how much more is involved than mere repression of the rejected shadow – there is another person altogether, a sub-system which has assumed its own identity. For the purposes of Freud, who was interested in therapy, such an identity was not encouraged. It was the patient himself, not 'somebody' inside him, who emotionally relived past events.

What seem to have been very similar happenings were given different labels by Janet, with his interest in the phenomena of hysterical hypnosis. Janet's patient Irénè is remarkably similar to Breuer's Anna O. She abreacted too, although Janet prefers to talk of automatism and somnambulism. Whatever the label, Irénè in her somnambulistic and dissociated state emotionally relived the events relating to the death of her mother. Much of the time she seemed callous and insensitive, emotionally apathetic and unconcerned. Yet occasionally her automatism (what Janet calls 'a system of emancipated thoughts') would take over, and the distressing repressed events would be relived. Whether we use the Freudian terminology of abreaction, or Janet's words, the actual behaviour involved seems very similar. Differences between Irénè and Anna O. could easily be overstated, for purely linguistic reasons.

There are few things left to which mental life has not so far been likened. Analogies have their legitimate place in scientific exposition and explanation. Observation of the activity of a pump seems to have assisted Harvey to his understanding of blood circulation; the coral reefs of the South Pacific helped Darwin to his more general theory of evolution by natural selection. As the psychologist Spearman has argued, there are limitations to creative human thinking: we observe sets of relations within one field and then apply them to another. The results of new observations may thus result in a fresh orientation and a new model.

I suspect that the old concept of 'dissociation' and related ideas such as 'co-consciousness', 'multiple personality', 'personality sub-systems' and 'dissociations of everyday life' have life in them yet. They can lead to a fresh examination of some mental events that psychoanalysis has, on the whole, neglected. Freud and psychoanalysis in their heyday provided exactly this kind of reorientation, and with it a new language with which to describe psychological events. That language has often been misunderstood. It has also involved temptations to reify – most of us find if difficult not to personify the 'ego, id and superego' as three little men inside the brain! The concept of 'the unconscious' readily arouses concrete imagery, and we need to remind ourselves that there is no such place. These terms are constructs, words to label complex events. They have served their uses, and when not misused will continue to function as tools of analysis, as a means to the end of scientific understanding.

In seeking to explain that motivation is complex, Freud and Breuer used many analogies: I have found no fewer than twenty-three in *Studies on Hysteria* alone. Some of these analogies, like those of Janet and Morton Prince, are spatial. In one place Freud and Breuer refer to the 'defile' of consciousness — a narrow pathway which allows psychological content to pass into the consciousness, 'cut up, as it were, into pieces or strips'. Freud adds that anyone with a craving for yet more similes may sensibly at this point think of the process of understanding unconscious mental life as one of sorting out a 'Chinese puzzle'. Elsewhere Freud and Breuer liken the psychiatrist coping with hysterical neurosis to the physician confronting an epidemic: when treated in one place it crops up elsewhere. In discussing repression they use the analogy of a foreign body in a living tissue. Electric lighting systems, the construction of multi-storey buildings and methods of translating pictographic script – all these come in, and more. Freud refers to buried cities, the mysterious movements of the Knight in a game of chess, the unlocking of a door.

Some of Freud's metaphors have lasted. I suspect that the familiar image of undesirable characters locked away has been misused. This notion of repression as involving a total forgetting and then a sudden emergence into conscious awareness (through hypnotism or free association) may well apply to hysteria patients. It seems less relevant to the psychology either of normal people or of some other patients, many of whom may be perfectly conscious (or pre-conscious) of their memories and motivational systems – their problem is much more that they are unable to interconnect them. The notion of mental systems, logic-tight or amnesic barriers which divide, and ways of re-connecting, merits re-examination. But this is only a more wordy way of saying that we should again ponder over the theme of 'dissociation revisited'.

11
Automatism and the
Language of Psychology

They have no conscious minds such as we say we have, and
certainly no introspections . . . They were noble automatons
who knew not what they did.

Julian Jaynes

In a study of the origins of consciousness, Julian Jaynes (1976)
questions the notion of a smooth and continuous process of
evolution in the human mind. In his opinion there was a
radical change once it was discovered that speech could be
recorded: with written language emerged consciousness, and
the capacity for introspective awareness. To illustrate the difference between the oral and the graphic traditions, Jaynes
cites Homer and the Hebrew prophets. The prophets, he
argues, in spite of their name, had little to say about the future;
they were men inspired by a divine message, which they de-
livered to their people. Their response to what modern psychology would call their autonomous imagery was to see it as
the voice of their god speaking within them. The Greek and
Trojan warriors of Homer's *Iliad* behave in much the same
way. Jaynes is impressed by the absence of thoughtful delibera-
tion, individual motivation and introspective awareness in
these 'noble automatons'. In a sense, he says, it could be said
that the Trojan war was 'directed by hallucinations'. Again
and again what we would see as the workings of human motivation are personified by Homer – and seen as such by his
protagonists – as the promptings of a god or goddess. These
divine beings demand obedience, much as do the 'voices' of the
modern psychotic, and this leaves little room for self-analysis.

Jaynes labels this Homeric mentality *the bicameral mind*. His

theory that introspective consciousness only emerged through
the breakdown of this way of seeing things is of considerable
interest to the study of dissociation – particularly when we
realize that the bicameral mind can still be found today in
certain individuals. Among other things, he examines the
growth of language through simile, metaphor and analogy.
The way we speak, and therefore think, about mental life is
largely dependent upon metaphor from physical experience:
for example, we see with our eyes, but we also 'see' the point of
an argument, establish a new 'viewpoint' and gain 'illumination' after grappling with the 'obscure'. The whole history of
psychology is filled with analogies. Plato was one of the first
theorists to describe the human personality in terms of a
hierarchy, and Freud was not the last. Today we have many
more systems to draw upon – television, photography, elec-
tronics, holography, nuclear physics, all these and more can
help us to describe ourselves in increasingly subtle and vivid
terms. We can label, discriminate, classify, possibly even
explain, and even in our everyday talk we are much better
equipped than Homer's heroes were to talk about our personal
lives. (Interestingly, however, since it supports Jayne's theory,
Homer's later epic *The Odyssey* shows a much greater awareness
of individual motivation – the breakdown of the bicameral
mind had already begun.)

Morton Prince writes of the mind's structure as 'a complex
integration of systems into one composite whole . . . the mind is
a composite of a lot of little minds, each concerned, however,
with its own business and its own interest and aim.' Even today
many societies, or pockets of society, and many individuals
attribute divine or diabolical reality to these 'little minds'. On
the whole, despite Jung and Freud and their successors, even
those of us who do not react to our mental sub-systems in this
way tend to ignore their 'message'. We mostly fall short of the
wisdom of the Senoi, who treat their children's dreamlives as
something to be learned from.

If our standpoint is naturalistic rather than supernatural,

the psychology of motivation can tell us a great deal about our 'little minds'. At this point I should like to draw attention to the work of an eighteenth-century moral philosopher with peculiar insight into these processes. In his *Sermons on Human Nature* (1729), Bishop Joseph Butler drew an analogy between the components of the human body and the parts of the human personality. Like our physical state, what Butler called our inward structure is 'not simple or uniform but a composition of various passions, appetites and affections, together with rationality'. Merely to list these parts is not enough; we need to study their functioning in relation to the total structure. Many years before Gestalt psychology, Butler recognized that a complex structure such as the personality is more than the sum of its parts.

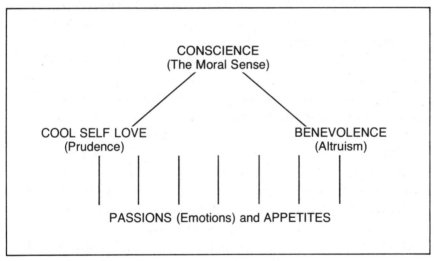

Joseph Butler's View of the Personality and its Motivation.

For Butler, the personality is a hierarchy integrated under the command of a moral sense called 'conscience', which functions in close relation to two major subordinates – benevolence (or altruism) and cool self love (or prudence). At the bottom of the hierarchy are the passions/emotions and the appetites; fear and hunger are typical representatives. These passions and appetites should not be confused with cool self love. The object of fear is escape, the object of hunger is food: either may come into sharp conflict with cool self love (a principle which closely resembles what Freud was later to call the Reality Principle). Cool self love guides actions in the direction of long-term self interest which may differ markedly from satisfaction of immediate impulses, passions or appetites. Butler therefore challenges the theory of egoism – the theory that all conduct is at bottom self-interested – on the grounds that it is psychologically incorrect. He also effectively demolishes the theory of hedonism, the view that man is motivated by pursuit of pleasure and avoidance of unpleasure. It may not have been as evident to the bicameral mind of Achilles as it is to us today, and as it was to Butler, that anger leads to many impulses and actions wholly contrary to self interest and long-term personal welfare. In the case of 'learned appetites' or addictions, for example, it is particularly plain that alcohol, tobacco and opiate drugs may assume precedence not only over self-interest but even over survival. The distinction which Freud was to make between the Pleasure Principle (immediate impulse-satisfaction) and the Reality Principle takes full account of these complexities of multiple motivation.

Butler's second major principle, alongside cool self love, is benevolence. This motivates us to take account of the welfare of other people. There is no necessary conflict between benevolence and prudence; on the contrary they often dictate similar conduct. Nor do either necessarily conflict with conscience, which approves or disapproves of conduct in terms of 'right' and 'wrong'. Butler likens the relations of conscience with the other propensities of the personality to those of a good headmaster with a well-run school: he can absent himself for a time, confident that he will not return to find anarchy. In other words, Butler views human virtue as yet another area in which habit reigns. There are exceptions (the people we would today call psychopaths, with no conscience at all), but apart from them it is a mere matter of fact that most ordinary citizens do not have to struggle daily with impulses to rob children of their possessions or assault innocent bystanders.

Obviously Butler's analysis of the personality and its motivational sub-systems has its limitations: it does not, for example, help us to understand the vicious, the mentally deranged sadist, the fanatic, the self-tormented. But it throws considerable light on the behaviour of more normal human beings. Butler had a profound understanding of the ways in which the different motivational systems of the personality may conflict and conspire. Like Freud he was also fully aware that any one principle may function to excess. Self love can and does overcome conscience. Some people are imprudently, even aggressively, kind. Others exhibit what Anna Freud was later to call pathological forms of 'altruistic surrender'; we have, after all, a responsibility to take ourselves seriously too, even if others also matter.

Butler was of course by no means the first to understand the sub-systems of the personality and the phenomena of multiple motivation. Many writers before him had revealed some uncomfortable truths. It was Hamlet's hatred, not his altruism, that restrained him from murdering the king at prayer. Men at prayer go straight to heaven. Hamlet was not indecisive, he was malicious: he was prepared to wait until the king himself was engaged in some evil deed, since this would ensure his punishment in afterlife. Romeo tempts the impoverished apothecary to sell him poison. In his wretchedness the man agrees, but he says 'my poverty, but not my will, consents'. Sheer necessity determines his agreement, and Butler's 'conscience' is pushed aside.

In due course, Freud gave his powerful endorsement to the principle of multiple motivation, but his psychoanalytic theory has some surprising weaknesses. Alexander Shand, the first Secretary of the British Psychological Society, raised a substantial criticism which is worth repeating since psychoanalytic theory does not yet seem to have answered it. Shand argued that psychoanalysis had not produced an adequate description of human emotional life, since it failed to distinguish between emotions and sentiments. For Shand, sentiments are complex habits of emotions allowing for a variety of specific emotional responses to the object in question. For example, anger and hate are typical emotions, while love and hate are typical sentiments: we can feel extremely angry with someone we love, without in fact losing that original sentiment.

Just as Shand, McDougall and their British followers had formulated the notion of the *sentiment*, the notion of the *complex* emerged from Europe. The name was used to describe an 'emotionally toned' system of ideas, and some psychologists treated the two concepts as synonymous. In 1922 a symposium of the British Psychological Society took place in Manchester. Its aim was to examine the structure of human emotional life. Specifically, it sought to determine whether or not psychology needed both concepts. It emerged that it did.

What is a complex? One contributor to the symposium, A. G. Tansley, pointed out that the word is used widely in science, to refer to objects dealt with as a group: a geographer speaks of a mountain complex, a biologist of a cell complex. The term had been brought into psychology by Jung, who applied it to an 'emotionally toned system of ideas' such as love or religious faith. Another contributor, C. S. Myers, described complexes as distinguished by 'surprise, irrationality and unpredictability'. Some contributors were prepared to identify complexes with repressed sentiments, others were not. One of the most interesting papers was presented by Professor T. H. Pear, the host psychologist at Manchester University. He argued that we need the two terms, sentiment and complex, to describe respectively the 'tidy' and the 'untidy' aspects of habitual emotional life. He refused to identify complexes as repressed sentiments, since many of our major sentiments involve 'not a little repression' – for example, we easily forget the faults of those we love and the virtues of those we hate, and this happens in relation to religious or political beliefs just as much as with individuals.

Pear made use of several analogies to communicate his

argument. He compared sentiments to tidy gardens tended by skilled gardeners. He likened them to music, as opposed to random noise – a good analogy, since people's emotional preferences are as pronounced and as much at variance with those of other people as their tastes in music, and passionate disagreement can arise in both cases. Pear also compared sentiments to well-designed switchboards. However, he reminded his audience, just as sophisticated electrical systems and well-kept gardens can deteriorate, so may a sentiment change into a complex, with dangerous live wires – the potential for emotional explosion – all over the place. What starts out as a moderate dislike of cats can turn into a complex about them; what starts out as love of one's country can turn into nationalist obsession; what starts out as love of God or allegiance to a political creed can turn into a mania.

In Shand's own view there are four basic emotions: joy, sorrow, fear and anger. Positive sentiments like love, liking and respect dictate a range of sympathetic emotional responses; there is joy in the presence of the object, regret at his prolonged absence, fear in the event of danger to him and anger in his defence. Negative sentiments dictate the opposite. Our actions, of course, may be more complicated than our reactions. We may, for example, hesitate to say or do what we really feel like saying or doing, for ethical reasons, or from guilt. Following Freud, Sir Cyril Burt was later to argue that all sentiments are 'ambivalent' in this way: love may be complicated by a latent resentment at the power the love-object has over one, and even our response to people we dislike can be contradictory. The ambivalence of human sentiment has been a favourite target for cynics and wits. The *Maxims* of la Rochefoucauld include the following: 'in the misfortunes of our dearest friends we always find something not entirely unpleasing to us', and 'if we judge love by its usual effect it resembles hatred rather than friendship'. Burt makes too much of a generalization perhaps, but his is a salutory reminder that sentiments are not always 'pure'.

The human personality is to a large extent a set of emotional habits, including sentiments and complexes. We have our emotional allegiances and antipathies to individuals; we have our religious, political and social preferences; we have our moral sentiments; we have our self-regarding sentiments. McDougall in particular made much of the sentiment of self-regard as the integrating principle of the human personality. These emotional habits are important sources of motivational energy, and we recognize constantly in our dealings with other people that their emotional habits are the main clue to their behaviour, the main influence upon our own reactions to them and the main area where we can apply pressure. We make appeals to a man's altruism, to his prudence, to his conscience; but we make appeals also to his prejudices. Often we are dealing not with the whole personality but with some emotional system within it. Bernard Hart placed great emphasis on the logic-tight compartments which protect our emotional habits from conflicting outside evidence; Eugene Bleuler wrote that 'the complexes can actually acquire sub-personalities with some sort of independence of the psyche' (Bleuler 1916). An extreme emotional habit may exert such control over the personality, when aroused, that we may half believe that we are dealing with a quite different person. These intense, autonomous emotional systems can be quite dangerous when they assume moralized form.

Leaving aside for a moment these darker extremes, let us look at a more mundane phenomenon – what Morton Prince called 'language automatisms', in which language becomes organized into 'set phrases or formulas which tend to become automatic and labour-saving devices for the expression of thought'. This often happens when we are asked repeatedly about the same event; and we must all know at least one person who drives us mad with his predictable stories or opinions. Reactions to this relatively harmless sort of repetition range from reluctant listening through carefully planned avoidance to actual physical flight. However, it is not unknown for this impatience to lead to murder, in quite ordinary domestic circumstances! Emotional automatism is often the root-cause of conflict between man and man, and it can even produce conflict within the same individual. In the Beauchamp case B1 and B4 were completely incompatible, and Sally felt contempt for both of them. Eve Black's aversion for Eve White's husband was intense, and her hatred of Eve White's child was compatible with murderous impulses. Within more normal personalities self-hatred is not uncommon, although it rarely expresses itself in relations between two fully developed sub-personalities within the same organism.

In discussing the habitual aspects of human emotion William James too draws attention to their motivational power. He writes that 'things hot and vital to us today are cold tomorrow'. These 'hot' parts of the personality James sees as 'centres of dynamic energy'. Sometimes this heat 'may come to lie permanently within a given system . . . if the change be a religious one we call it conversion.' Many modern writers have discussed this phenomenon in the context of political belief, perhaps most noticeably in the case of conversion to communism. According to Arthur Koestler, such is the heat of political conviction, such the 'intellectual rapture' that the convert knows, that a 'new light seems to pour in from all directions' (Koestler 1954). In his own case he records a reorganization of the sentiments in which 'the whole universe falls into pattern like the stray pieces in a jigsaw puzzle'. Once converted he felt himself joined to a system of thought which explained all things and could cure all ills. From his intrapsychic conflicts he 'stepped from an intellectually open into an intellectually closed world'.

In recent years considerable research attention has been paid to the techniques of producing this sort of conversion of the sentiments through brainwashing. To take just one example, psychologists interviewed prisoners who collaborated with their captors during the Korean War. It transpired that their original loyalties were systematically undermined by rewards and punishments. This process of building up a new personality for political purposes is the darker side of what therapy can do for the multiple personality: we do well perhaps to remember that the same principles can be used to widely differing ends. In the Beauchamp case Sally was 'squeezed out' and the B1 and B4 personalities were integrated. The process is not unlike that described in Koestler's conversion – and interestingly Koestler expresses a very strong retrospective dislike of his former self. Converts are in fact notoriously intolerant. Koestler suggests that the last battle will be fought between the Marxists and the ex-Marxists. People familiar with converts of any kind will know just what he meant.

Some sub-systems of the personality exhibit a pathologically stable character. Extreme examples are to be found in the psychosis diagnosed as 'true paranoia'. One of the most famous cases of all time involved Daniel McNaghten, tried at the Old Bailey in 1843 for the murder of Edward Drummond, private secretary of Sir Robert Peel. It was a case of mistaken identity: McNaghten had intended to kill Peel. McNaghten emerged at the trial as a dignified, solitary man, who behaved outwardly as a law-abiding and respectable citizen. He was, however, obsessed with the notion that he was being persecuted by the Catholic Church. Sir Robert Peel had championed the cause of Irish emancipation, so obviously he and the Tory party must be part of the conspiracy. McNaghten's orientation to the events of the day was entirely clouded by emotion. His case, which gave rise to the McNaghten Rules, is historically and legally important; it also provides a reference point which may help us to understand some lesser manifestations of pathologically stable sub-systems.

It is possible to talk for quite a long time to a psychotic patient of this type before discovering this inner core of abnormality. Many people have mini-paranoid sub-systems in their prejudices, sentiments and other emotional habits. The pioneer of behaviourism in psychology, J. B. Watson, had much to say about this in his discussion of personality and its disturbance (Watson 1919). He suggests that therapists should inquire into the 'soured' aspects of a patient's mental life and into how he has adjusted to past failures. He refers to 'balancing factors' – components of the personality, ranging from religious faith to a sense of humour, which may have enabled a person to adjust to past failures and past mistakes. The word 'paranoia' refers to the personality in which an over-sensitive and disturbed sub-system is not making these adjustments. Such an individual is likely to be solitary, and to lack the friends and acquaintances who can moderate his or her distorted apprehensions of the world.

Another interesting case, less well known than McNaghten's, concerns one Lionel Terry, who in 1905 committed a murder in a street in Wellington, New Zealand. He chose as his victim an elderly Chinese. The police authorities were completely baffled as to the motive for the murder. The following day Terry walked into the Lambton Quay police station to inform a surprised police officer that he had taken the life of this man in an attempt to challenge the law of the country. At the trial Terry was found guilty with a strong recommendation to mercy on the grounds that he was not responsible: 'he was suffering from a craze caused by his intense hatred towards the mixing of British and alien races (*New Zealand Times*, 21 November 1905). Sentence of death was passed, but in fact Terry spent his life in various institutions, becoming probably the most famous patient in New Zealand psychiatric history. Terry is a perfect example of dangerous live wires. It transpired that he had served in the South African Mounted Police and been wounded in the Matabele war: at some point in this experience, it seems, the seeds were sown of a racial complex which would erupt later to the point of murder in the life of an otherwise civilized and intelligent man.

The distinction between delusion and belief is as difficult to draw as that between hallucination and other forms of imagery. Pathologically stable belief systems can be untypical of the personality as a whole, and they may be locked away in

logic-tight compartments. Compartmentalization of one sort
or another is, of course, characteristic of the human mind.
Freud called it 'isolation'. At its best we encounter it in the
impartiality of the judge or the objectivity of the scientist; but
we frequently encounter it in less admirable form in the seemingly inevitable insensitivities of everyday life, where we cannot afford to be all things to all men. In his book *The Mask of
Sanity*, published in 1941, Cleckley writes of this process of
compartmentalization in relation to the prejudices of the normal personality – only he calls it 'dissociation'. Our prejudices
can survive even when they go against everything else in our
personalities. Cleckley deduces that a prejudice 'is isolated
from ordinary conscious thinking, or logical reasoning. A dissociation has taken place.' Such inconsistency seems to be
fairly typical of mankind; what we see in dual or multiple
personality cases is to some extent simply the same thing in
exaggerated form.

In the final chapter I shall be much concerned with what the
psychologist Henry Murray calls 'ambitendencies'. These are
the paradoxically opposing personal attributes we may find in
the same person. Two illustrations may be taken from a single
issue of the London *Sunday Times* (6 August 1978). One passage
quotes D. H. Lawrence's description of Sir Osbert Sitwell: 'his
eyes, at the same time bold and frightened, assured and uncertain, revealed his nature . . . he was often offensively supercili-
ous, and again modest and self-effacing, almost tremulous.'
Another declares that Alexander Pope 'could adopt opposed
attitudes on almost any topic': on one occasion the poet
responded to a tragedy involving two young people by writing
two epitaphs, one religious, the other indecent.

We have already noted the great interest shown in dissociative phenomena by both literature and science in the early part
of the century. In *The Discovery of the Unconscious* (1970), Ellenberger draws attention to the upsurge during that period of a
literature concerned with 'subtler descriptions of the many
facets of human personality . . . their interplay'. He cites in

particular Marcel Proust, with his interest in the fact that the personality can be 'composed of many little egos, distinct though side by side'. Ellenberger notes that hypnotism 'provided the first model of the human mind as a double ego'; and in discussing the multiple personality he recommends the notion that the personality is 'like a matrix from which whole sets of sub-personalities could emerge and differentiate themselves'. He discusses also the important question of what can happen once we give names to certain phenomena; sub-personalities may develop spontaneously, but they may also be influenced by suggestion, exaggerated by investigators and established more firmly through personification. Ellenberger quotes Janet's observation that 'once baptized the unconscious personality is more clear and definite; it shows its psychological traits more clearly'. Earlier we saw how a hallucinated patient may name, and thus personify, his hallucinatory 'voices'; Ellenberger reminds us that even someone who simply keeps a diary over a long period may develop something of a dual personality. Ellenberger is interested in the links between the normal and the more extreme manifestations of what he calls 'polypsychism'; this model is well worth looking at.

Among our many 'polypsychic' inconsistencies or 'ambitendencies', we humans are subject to changes of mood. Some useful introspections into this phenomenon are provided by the great nineteenth-century explorer, Sir Richard Burton. In *Pilgrimage to El Medina and Mecca*, published in 1853, Burton takes us into the consciousness of the dedicated traveller. He tells how such a person, after a journey, may settle down to become 'the most domestic of men': he enjoys to the full such benefits of civilization as uninterrupted sleep in a comfortable bed, and regular meals. But time passes and something happens; something inside him takes over; 'the man wants to wander and must do so, or he shall die'. Of himself, Burton reports that after a month of rest in Alexandria he noticed 'the approach of the enemy' – 'I surrendered.'

Burton writes as if the upsurge of motivation arises

spontaneously from inside. His observations are fascinating, but we must not let him discount entirely the influence of external stimuli. In a book dedicated to Morton Prince, E. B. Holt (1931) provides an interesting analysis of the influence of external perceptual factors on motivational change. As he says, there are many 'mild annoyers' in the environment (the sound of a waterfall nearby, the 'din and odour of factories and cities'); these often exercise a great influence over people who live in the vicinity, and may even become vital for their mental health. Distracted by them initially, a man may in time cease to notice them consciously – but he may be curiously troubled by their absence at some later stage. The rocking of a ship does not annoy the sailor, it positively sustains him; such men 'suffer, sometimes acutely, if obliged to remain ashore'. There would certainly have been many perceptual stimuli in Alexandria to remind Burton of the journey to Mecca that awaited him. Consider Holt's keen yachtsman, working at his desk: a sudden combination of sunshine with a fresh breeze will 'stimulate the man's whole yachting complex'; there arises in him 'an unaccountable "mood" or "desire" to go yachting which may demoralize his whole working day'.

Motivational changes may be prompted by external stimuli of which we are barely conscious at the time. Freud had an interesting case in this context, which appeared at first to support the notion of telepathy. A psychoanalyst and his wife were dining in a New York restaurant; suddenly he remarked to her that he wondered how 'Dr R.' was getting on in Pittsburgh: she looked at him in astonishment, and said that she had been about to say the same thing. Only later did they realize that there was a man at another table who strongly resembled 'Dr R.': sub-conscious perception of him had set in motion the same train of thought in both minds. Both Edgar Allan Poe and Conan Doyle made use of such pseudo-telepathic incidents: they introduced situations in which one man was able by association of ideas to enter into the thoughts of another, and interrupt that thought with an appropriate remark. We must be careful not to underestimate the influence of perception of what appear to be autonomous thought-processes. To illustrate from my own observations, I was walking along a street in Aberdeen once with a psychologist colleague. The colleague told me that she suddenly found herself thinking about a 'pink griffin', and asked herself 'what on earth put that into my mind?' We were soon able to solve the mystery. She remembered seeing a little earlier the emblem of the 'Phoenix Insurance Company' above an office. The perception was marginal to consciousness, but strong enough to set up the associative train of thought. As such cases as these illustrate, it is important to remember that behaviour which seems to stem spontaneously from organism may in fact be elicited by some environmental stimulation, however marginal.

In the 1920s, J. R. Kantor – a major psychologist who worked on the frontier between psychology and economics – emphasized the need to study 'the mutual interaction of the organism and the environment'. He stressed the need to study both the stimuli and the reactions. Modern personality psychology is increasingly realizing the fruitfulness of this approach. The research literature as summarized by Bowers (1973) from the United States and Ekehammar (1974) from Sweden stressed this 'Person × Situation' equation. It has proved to be more powerful as a basis for prediction than the isolated study of either individual or situational differences. A major contributor to this standpoint – now well supported by experimental research – was Henry Murray. Murray, successor to Morton Prince as Director of the Harvard Psychological Clinic, viewed the problems of personality as an interaction of two sets of forces. On the one hand are the motives or needs – sub-systems conceived of as forces from within the personality. On the other are 'press' – the forces from the environment. In the chapter to follow I shall attempt an application of Murray's viewpoint, to both the integration and the distintegration of the personality.

12
Personality and
Its Sub-Systems

The two opposing needs may be termed an ambitendency
... A man acts like Napoleon at home, but in business is
obedient and servile ... Needs may come into conflict with
each other within the personality, giving rise when prolonged to harassing spiritual dilemmas.

Henry Murray

For some purposes the human personality may be viewed as an
integrated whole, behaving within an overall environment. For
others, however, it is fruitful to recognize the component sub-
systems of the personality and the fact that they may be activated by specific environmental forces. Here, as in so much
else, individuals vary. Degree of personality integration (an
attribute which Murray labels 'conjunctivity') is an important
variable in the normal as well as in the pathological personality. Ordinary sentiments, for example, may be more or less
consistent with one another, and they may give rise to conflict
not only between different people but also within the same
person. At the same time, as the psychoanalysts have shown,
there are many mechanisms of self-deception (repression is the
obvious example) which can blur insight into these conflicts
and inconsistencies.

Individuals vary enormously in the amount of insight they
have into their inconsistencies. In Murray's opinion,
psychologists do not always help: in personality tests, for
example, we calculate an average, but this should never be
allowed to 'obscure an ambitendency'. Consider, for instance,
Sir Richard Burton – keen explorer, but also keen enthusiast
for the comforts of civilization. If we average such an indi-

vidual, 'the final score will put the individual near the mid line, just where he never was' (Murray 1938).

Murray's emphasis is on the interaction of internal motivation and external, environmental pressure. The major internal motivators are a repertoire of needs, which are activated by stimulus situations defined as 'that part of the total environment to which the creature attends and reacts'. These influences may be supportive, restrictive, amusing, threatening, etc. In everyday language we classify environmental forces in such terms as 'that hurts', 'this comforts', 'this annoys', 'this amuses'. These environmental 'press' (plural), as he calls them, Murray (1943) classifies in the broad categories of positive and negative, mobile and immobile. He also gives names to specific forms of need and press. For example, individuals exhibit varying degrees of 'need aggression' (n. aggression), and situations varying degrees of 'press aggression' (p. aggression).

An illustration may be taken from the psychology of childhood – an area where there has been too much emphasis on 'what psychologists say'. Psychologists may seem to be in the business of making generalizations; but they are emphatic that individuals differ, and children are no exception. In discussing the issue of punishment of children, Sir Cyril Burt draws attention to what Murray would call 'press punishment'. Burt argues that there are under-punished, over-punished and inconsistently punished children: each child may require different handling, depending on his past punishment history. To illustrate further from Murray, an individual may exhibit strong n. dominance: his personal motivational systems drive him to impose his will on others. Someone else may be on the receiving end of p. dominance from others. We begin to understand personalities when we settle down to the study of such needs and such press. In adult life, for example, a given person may exhibit markedly different behaviour at home and at work because the press of the two situations may be quite different: a submissive wife and a bullying employer will almost see him as two different people.

Some applications of these concepts may usefully be made to the phenomena which have concerned us in preceding chapters. It has already been noted that there are many circumstances, many forms of press, that may elicit hallucination in individuals who do not otherwise hallucinate. These press include subjection to conditions of sensory deprivation, and the administration of a hallucinogenic drug; the press of sleep deprivation is also effective if sufficiently extended. As regards the polypsychic natures of Miss Beauchamp and May Naylor, it is clear that their different sub-personalities had different needs. It is evident that both Eve White and Sybil Dorsett exhibited, to a marked degree, Murray's n. abasement, and perhaps also a measure of masochism. We may note in this context another multiple-personality case, G. E. Morselli's Elena, reported in the 1930s. Two sub-systems were involved, one of which spoke French, the other Italian (the 'Italian' personality spoke French with an Italian accent, and vice versa). Morselli observed that the 'Italian' personality exhibited the most normality, and his therapy was designed to make this the dominant one. Of interest is the 'press' involved in this therapy: he sought to strengthen the Italian personality system by getting his patient to read aloud long passages from Dante in Italian.

In the Sybil Dorsett case, the rather submissive personality of the original Sybil makes sense if we remember the strong press of the physical cruelty she had suffered at the hands of her disturbed mother. This press gave rise to two things: the depleted personality of Sybil herself, and the emergence of other more robust personalities. Both Peggy Lou and Vicky were very much better able to look after themselves than the original Sybil. In Vicky we note the strong motivation to care for, and mother, the baby personality, Ruthie. She exhibited what Murray would call n. nurturance. The prevailing social pressures of the family situation and of the town in which Sybil lived were the subject of dry comment by Marcia and Vanessa: they had had to develop a sense of humour to survive.

Some of the n. and equivalent p. of Murray's finite list derive from everyday language. Other names, such as n. or p. counteraction (making up for failure by trying again) he invented. Others again derive from the literature of psychology. Spanish Maria (Chapter 3) in her secondary personality, exhibited to a greater extent than in her primary personality such needs as n. narcissism and n. exhibitionism: the press to which she had been subjected in her early life was such as to discourage her self-assertive and sexual needs, so a secondary personality of a markedly different kind emerged, to foster their development. For the purpose of my own analysis of dissociation I shall draw on Murray's list of needs and press, but I shall also when necessary make use of others of my own. It is important to remember, for example, that therapy itself is a form of press; all the various belief-systems, amongst psychologists themselves just as much as anyone else, contribute different sorts of press. Consider Hélène Smith (Chapter 5). Her psychologist investigator, Flournoy, was himself highly sceptical of her colourful incarnations; but, as a popular medium in Geneva, she would undoubtedly have received much reinforcement from those ordinary citizens who wanted to believe in her imaginative fantasies.

The study of specific environmental pressures and their role in the expression and development of specific personal needs can tell us a great deal about the various manifestations of multiple personality. Some psychologists have sought an explanation of the major psychoses in the circumstances of the home and family. Some schizophrenic patients have undoubtedly had 'schizophrenogenic' parents: it may not wholly explain the ensuing psychosis, but negative press from parents certainly does not seem to assist normal development of the personality. There is no equivalent word for the outside pressures which may foster a sense of persecution, so I shall simply speak of 'paranoid press'. This may stem less from the actual situation as an objective reality than from imaginative interpretation of it, or even misperception. By way of illustration, let us look at an early experiment by the Victorian scientist Sir Francis Galton.

Galton wanted to see if he could find out what persecutory states of mind felt like. During a walk through London he conducted an experiment on himself. What he did was simply to imagine that everybody he met was a spy. His experiment succeeded beyond his expectations. Galton records how, after a walk of about a mile and a half, he reached the cab stand in Piccadilly. There he found that 'every horse on the stand seemed to be watching me, either with pricked ears, or disguising its espionage.' Galton adds, 'hours passed before this

RESPONSE TO ENVIRONMENTAL PRESS

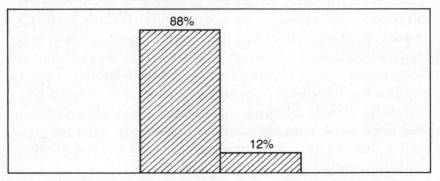

Behaviour of 50 consecutive pedestrians in relation to a ladder. Of these, 88% (44 individuals) observed the superstition and walked round, and only a minority defied the superstition and walked under.

uneasy sensation wore off, and I felt I could only too easily re-establish it'. Readers may like to try out similar ordeals on themselves. A variant is to sit in a restaurant, and work oneself and companions into a state of 'the waiter doesn't like us; he won't come and serve us; what has he got against us?' I have found that a mildly paranoid state of mind can readily be induced in such circumstances.

Galton made other attempts to combine such injections of fantasy and imagery with perception of objective reality. For example, he set out to enter into the mind of the idolator by developing in himself a sentiment of reverence for the figure of Punch. He reports that he succeeded. A small experiment of my own may be cited to illustrate superstition-inducing press. A ladder propped casually across a pavement was a sufficiently strong environmental force to induce the majority of pedestrians to walk round it, not under it. I acknowledge, however that this number may have included many who did not entirely believe in the superstition. Obviously the states of mind of the people concerned, their inner circumstances, have considerable importance. Studies of overt behaviour of this ladder-superstition type might usefully be made with students on their way to examinations, say, or couples going to their weddings. The interactions of need and press are not everything. Important also are other sub-systems of the personality, its past history, and its present state of mind and preoccupations.

The concepts of need and press may be applied to some interesting observations made by W. H. R. Rivers in his psychiatric work on war neurosis cases from World War I. He found that two different types of psychiatric syndrome occurred: conversion hysteria on the one hand, and anxiety neurosis on the other. He also observed a strong tendency for the hysterias to affect private soldiers, and for anxiety neurosis to be confined to officers. He related this to the different situations in which the two types of men were placed. To use Murray's terms, the private soldier was subject to a strong press to obey orders immediately and without question. Such a press fostered the development of suggestibility, a trait closely associated with hysteria. The needs expressed themselves through physical symptons, like blindness, deafness and paralysis: these achieved the goal of enabling the men to be withdrawn from the fear-stimulating situations of trench warfare. Very different were the officers. Their status forbade them to show fear in any shape or form. Since it could not be expressed, it had to be repressed, and the result was anxiety neurosis rather than hysterical symptoms and signs.

In considering an emotion such as fear it is important to note that the emotion is provoked by something. The provoking circumstances may have little to do with reality, and everything to do with the outlook of the person concerned. This emphasis on the difference between the environment as perceived, and the environment as it is, forms part of Murray's theory. The perceived environment is the product of interaction between the person and his physical surroundings. That person has a history, a system of sentiments and other attributes; he has many characteristics which may lead him to misperceive. This leads Murray to distinguish two different types of press. He distinguishes 'alpha press' (actual reality) from 'beta press' (perceived reality). A great deal depends on the personality, its expectancies and other attributes as the possibilities of misperception. To a large extent psychologists have to rely on 'beta press', the subject's own narrative, although we can sometimes check the realities of 'alpha press' from external sources. To return to the emotions, many people are provoked to anger by insults and humiliations which seem to have no basis in reality as witnessed by any impartial bystander. Conversely, I have watched the behaviour of people in situations of considerable danger without realizing it; they were not frightened.

As we have seen, people can be terrified when there is nothing there. Anticipation, anxiety and superstition combined with solitude, darkness and human imaginings can be very effective as beta press towards fear. Galton was an experienced traveller, in fact an explorer of parts of Africa. In his *Art of Travel* (1876) he discusses actual and fancied dangers, as perceived by the tent dweller and by the man used to the bivouac. When there is a night alarm the man used to tents will cling to the fancied security of his tent walls and his lanterns. By contrast the man used to the bivouac 'runs naturally into the dark for safety, just like a wild animal'. Some of us will be able to confirm Galton's observations on this point from personal experience. On one occasion I was alone overnight in a remote part of New Zealand during a storm. During the early part of the night I huddled in my shelter around my candles and torch; these gave me security from the surrounding darkness. Later I slept. When I awoke during the night I found that I had become adjusted to the environment of darkness, and was comfortable and secure without light.

Koestler (1954) has some sharp insights into some even more curious ways in which our state of mind may control our response to environmental press. At one time he experienced acute poverty and semi-starvation, in Haifa, for the whole of one year, and during one particularly hungry period be would often refuse invitations to meals, on the pretext of being busy. When he did accept, he felt bound to refuse second helpings. Koestler comments on the absence of accounts of hunger in literature, and suggests that civilized man needs 'to cover up his hunger as a naked man covers his sex'. When you are hungry the mere offer of food can lead to semi-persecutory thoughts. Quite apart from anything else, there is the question of morale: it is easier to accept a gift when one has money in one's pocket, and thus the potential to return the compliment.

To assess a person's personality solely in terms of personality traits is to leave out some important dynamics. One of the standard psychological tests seeks to place the individual on a scale of intraversion/extraversion – here too the final score may put him 'just where he never was'. In tests of this kind, the subject often feels like saying 'but it depends on the circumstances'. It certainly seems that we should take the 'person × situation' equation somewhat more into account. A given individual may be highly introverted on one occasion, and highly extraverted on another. Press may be extraverting: in the benevolent atmosphere of a wedding reception the most consistent introvert can surprise his spouse with a witty speech; on the other hand there are some situations which will defeat the most enthusiastic extravert.

Studies have been made of the ways in which Murray's 'needs' may be translated either into overt action or into fantasy. Sometimes there is a direct relation, sometimes there is an inverse one, and sometimes there is no relation at all. An individual's fantasies – in such areas, say, as achievement and sexual conquest – may find minimal expression in overt action.

In some of the classic cases of multiple personality, human imagining activity may play an important part in the development of a secondary personality. It also plays its part in lesser dissociative phenomena like crystal-gazing, automatic writing and artistic creation. Such activity may be a compensation for inadequate overt expression in action. Moreover as 'depth psychology' – psychoanalysis and its derivatives – has shown us, some strong emotional preoccupations do not even reach this level of conscious recognition. They are repressed and, as we have seen, may form the nucleus of major or minor dissociated systems.

Let us take a closer look at these emotions of ours. On occasions, an emotion like rage or terror may take us over completely; its domination may completely silence those principles of motivation which Butler called conscience, prudence and altruism. Anger itself was described by the Roman writer Horace as 'short madness'; St Augustine called it a 'weed'. Like all the other emotions, however, anger does not erupt of itself – it is in some way provoked, and this provocation arises through perception of situations, that is through beta rather than alpha press. Some of my own earlier research was on the anger emotions: anger itself, rage and indignation. This work led me to distinguish two types of anger-inducing press. Anger may be provoked either by a thwarting of our needs or by some threat to the personality itself and what it values; I therefore distinguished N-situations (need situations) from P-situations (personality situations). These two different kinds of press appeared to produce two different kinds of anger. The N-situation anger tended to be hot-blooded, of brief duration and directed towards the destruction (or at least removal) of the obstacle to need-satisfaction. By contrast, P-situation anger was long-enduring, coldly purposeful and revenge-orientated. Obviously, anger of the N-situation kind is not harmless; on the contrary, it may result in that 'short madness' which may temporarily turn a normal human being into a dangerous automaton. P-situation anger appears to be different. The aim of such anger is to retaliate: once hurt or humiliated oneself, there is a desire to inflict the same on someone else. This may be pursued at the expense of prudence, even to the point of self-destructive activity.

When Moses established the social rule 'an eye for an eye, a tooth for a tooth', this was in a sense 'the beginning of morality'; it at least set limits on the expression of revengeful anger. Some instances of such anger have been collected by Parry (1968) in his study of a neglected area of road-safety research. Many of the cases of such anger in Parry's *Aggression on the Road* are frightening. One of the drivers interviewed told how he drove his car into the other man's: 'I would have smashed his face in too . . . I'm sorry about my own car being damaged, but it was worth it.' Some people admitted edging other cars off the road out of sheer righteous disapproval. One told in interview how he backed into another car: 'That stopped him, but it ruined my car's rear wing and lights.' Personally, I still feel a measure of revengeful indignation against the drunken motorist who, two nights ago as I write, swerved his car and nearly ran me down.

An interesting feature of negative sentiments like hatred and contempt, and their associated emotion, anger, is their tendency to assume moralized forms. Alexander Shand (1914) formulated an interesting principle relating to one important source of inconsistency in human behaviour. According to the principle of Relative Ethics, although we have general moral standards (our conscience, superego or moral sentiments) we make 'moral' exceptions with those we dislike, hate or feel coldly angry against. History records only too many tragic cases. I shall take one instance. How, for example, did the morally scrupulous Oliver Cromwell react when his own soldiers massacred some 3,000 Irish people after the fall of Drogheda? With guilt and remorse? On the contrary, in accord with his positive sentiments towards his soldiers, and his grief for their casualties, he reacted moralistically. He referred to the 'righteous judgment of God', and in accord with the relative ethics of his sentiments denied any right.to mercy to 'those hideous wretches who have soiled *their* hands with so much innocent blood'.

When powerful sentiments, accompanied by moralized emotion, assume precedence in our behaviour, an entirely different system seems to operate, often quite insulated from such principles as conscience, benevolence or even prudent self-preservation. The result is that seemingly normal people can act in a way which is wholly out of accord with their usual behaviour. In one American study, 25 per cent of the 1,000 people interviewed declared that they would personally support vigilante activities. As many as 10 per cent of these ordinary, middle-class Americans declared themselves willing to join an armed assault on anti-Vietnam-war protesters. Furthermore, no less than 41 per cent of them owned a gun, sometimes several. A gun in the hands of a righteously angry man – however respectable a citizen he ordinarily is – provides much justifiable cause for fear. Moralization can give powerful support to the logic-light functional systems of the personality.

It was while watching an all-in wrestling match that I first became convinced of the importance of Shand's principle of Relative Ethics. One wrestler had obeyed the rules, while the other had presistently used illicit tactics – these had mostly been overlooked by the referee. When the 'honest' wrestler came out on top and had the 'villain' wrestler at his mercy, a surge of moralized anger went through the audience. Many jumped to their feet and cried out, demanding that the 'honest' wrestler inflict maximum suffering, injury, even death on the 'villain'. I myself found it difficult not to identify with this demand for retributive justice. All-in wrestling was studied in 1967 by G. P. Stone (a psychiatrist) and R. A. Oldburg (a sociologist). They note the clear-cut distinction between 'good' and 'evil'. It is vital for the wrestler to build up a reputation as either a clean-wrestling hero or a foul-wrestling villain. The villains sometimes identify themselves by their dress, with masks or other devices. The audience comes along to see 'good' triumph over 'evil', much as the child does at a pantomime. They are equipped with well-established negative sentiments towards the villain and positive sentiments towards their hero, and neither disappoints them. The referee is there as much to 'overlook' as to enforce any rules (Stone and Oldburgh 1967). Upon enquiring into the composition of the typical audience, the investigators found an over-representation of women of low socio-economic status. Spectators seem generally to have regarded all-in wrestling as a kind of 'morality play' – a drama or spectacle representing the conflict between good and evil in simplified form.

The press which provokes emotion, and activates the sentiments, prejudices and complexes which we have talked about, is not confined to face-to-face situations. I have suggested elsewhere (McKellar 1968, 1977) that a distinction should be drawn between 'primary perception' (perceiving the event directly) and 'secondary perception' (watching a film, looking at a photograph, listening to a broadcast or recording): in secondary perception there is an intermediary between the perceiver and the thing perceived. Through the printed word, radio, photography, television and the film, we engage in a great deal of such secondary perception and it enormously enlarges our perceptual field. It is possible, for example, to become emotionally aroused about events one has never witnessed, in places one has never been to, even in times one doesn't live in; it is possible to develop strong sentiments about people one has never met, including those fictional characters who don't exist in any case. As for the controversial question of the influence of secondary perception on crime, this is now being studied with some concern.

Secondary perception through the media has had almost as dramatic an effect upon modern man as the breakdown of the bicameral mind had upon our post-Homeric ancestors. Writers and artists have recorded man's inhumanity for centuries, and we have painted pictures of our world almost since the world began – but with the arrival of photo-journalism in particular we now have to call the *whole* world our own. The emotional effect upon individual psyches has been incalculable.

The Penguin paperback was invented in 1935. By 1939 there was a radio in 75 per cent of homes in Britain – in good time for World War II. It was through radio that the American people learned of the bombing of Pearl Harbor. Television enabled Western viewers to form an opinion, one way or another, about the Vietnam war, and the killing of Lee Harvey Oswald by Jack Ruby was witnessed by millions of people. Secondary perception is all-important today both as a source of information and as a source of pressure. The media can arouse intense emotions, build stereotypes, inform, persuade, deceive, lead us into fantasy, lead us into crime, lead us into despair, make us laugh, make us cry.

What, then, of our private selves in this barrage of stimuli? In the circumstances, one might be forgiven for asking why the personality does not fall to pieces more often. Freud managed to take us beyond typology and beyond superstition to a more humane concern with individual lives. The polypsychic model, Murray's emphasis on man's relationship with his environment, all the studies of sub-systems in the normal as well as the abnormal personality – the dissociationist tradition should now take its rightful place beside the psychoanalytical in shaping the future of the science of psychology.

Glossary

Labels are all important in this area of psychology. Some of the terms explained below are my own; most are from the established vocabulary of psychology I have occasionally wished to correct misuses, e.g. the equation of somnambulism with nocturnal events only.

ABREACTION An emotional reliving (during psychoanalysis or other therapy) of an emotionally charged past event. The patient does more than merely talk emotionally, he relives the experience and expresses emotions similar to those experienced at the time. Resemblances may be noted between abreaction and spontaneous somnambulisms (q.v.) as discussed by Pierre Janet.

AFTER-SENSATION (sometimes *after-image*). The continuation of a sense experience (often, but not always, visual) after removal of the original stimulus: e.g. exposure to a well-illuminated red stimulus may give rise to an after-sensation in green (red's complementary colour).

ALTER EGO One's other self. It may be the REPRESSED and repudiated part of the psyche, what Jung calls 'the Shadow' (q.v.).

ALTERNATING PERSONALITY Temporary control of the personality by one sub-system until another sub-system takes over: e.g. the B1 and B4 sub-systems in the Beauchamp case.

AMNESIA Loss of memory. There may be amnesic barriers between the sub-systems in a FUGUE or a MULTIPLE PERSONALITY. Similar amnesic barriers, in post-hypnotic suggestions (q.v.) may divide the post-hypnotic personality from the hypnotic personality which receives the suggestion.

AUTOMATIC WRITING Writing that occurs without conscious intention or control, and without awareness of what is being written until it appears. It arises from some autonomous SUB-SYSTEM OF THE PERSONALITY – or, of course, from a supernatural source, depending on one's beliefs.

AUTONOMOUS IMAGERY Mental imagery in which the author lacks control over the content, occurrence and termination of such imagery: e.g. the imagery of a typical dream, HALLUCINATION or HYPNAGOGIC experience. Contrast CONTROLLED IMAGERY.

AUTOSCOPIC 1. autoscopic HALLUCINATION: hallucinating oneself – a rarity. 2. autonomous IMAGERY: imagery of oneself – a common phenomenon.

BODY IMAGE The impression each person has of his own body as a physical object in space, with spatially related parts. Body-image changes may occur in the HYPNAGOGIC state and with hallucinogens, and they may be induced hypnotically. The body images of the sub-systems in MULTIPLE PERSONALITY may differ in size, hair-colour and even gender.

CO-CONSCIOUSNESS Morton Prince's term for the co-existing secondary personality which has awareness of the sub-system which is in control of the organism. In the Beauchamp case, Sally was co-conscious and overlooked both B1 and B4, although they had no direct conscious awareness of her.

COMPLEX Term employed by Jung and others to refer to an emotionally toned system of ideas. It is used in psychoanalysis and has also been used by some British psychologists (e.g. Bernard Hart) as a synonym for SENTIMENT. Rivers identified complexes with 'repressed sentiments', but T. H. Pear argued that 'sentiment' and 'complex' are distinct.

CONTROLLED IMAGERY Mental imagery in which the author has voluntary control over content and adjustments to the imagery. Contrast AUTONOMOUS IMAGERY.

DISSOCIATED EMOTION Free-floating emotion in which the emotion is primary and the object or situation to which it is attached is secondary: e.g. in an hallucinogen experiment, a person in a depressed state has a HALLUCINATION; although his depression is primary he may be tempted to attribute the depression to the hallucination.

DISSOCIATION Sub-systems or aspects of the individual's personality divorce themselves from one another and, having broken off relations, maintain a life of their own with amnesic barriers between them in place of their usual connection. Many aspects of dreams, artistic inspiration, hallucination, alleged spirit possession and hypnotism may be interpreted as manifestations of dissociation.

DOMINANT SOMNAMBULISM A SOMNAMBULISM in which the secondary system assumes precedence and takes over from the primary personality system (Janet). Similar dominance may occur in FUGUES, HYPNOSIS and in MULTIPLE PERSONALITY.

DREAM BODY A neutral term used by van Eeden for the dreaming equivalent of the BODY IMAGE; it avoids the supernatural overtones of such a term as 'astral body'.

FALLING EXPERIENCE In the absence of an established one, I suggest this name for the common illusory impression of falling and then waking with a start in the hypnagogic state.

FUGUE A flight from one personal identity to another (often including physical travel), accompanied by AMNESIA for the previous identity: e.g. the Rev. Ansel Bourne.

HALLUCINATION An imagery experience of the auditory, visual or other sense modes, liable to be confused with a real perception. Hallucination is sometimes distinguished from 'pseudo-hallucination', in which insight is retained into the subjective origin of the experience. Spontaneous hallucinations are often auditory; visual hallucinations are more easily produced experimentally.

HIDDEN OBSERVER An experimentally produced co-conscious system (produced in Hilgard's experiments on pain) which is capable of introspective communications, e.g.through AUTOMATIC WRITING.

HYPNAGOGIC IMAGE Imagery of any sense mode, characteristically autonomous and sometimes of hallucinatory vividness, experienced in the drowsy state before sleep. It has been classified into the categories of (a) *perseverative*, when the sensory origins in past experience are obvious, and (b) *impersonal*, when such origins are difficult to trace and the images reveal a strange originality of their own.

HYPNOPOMPIC IMAGE Imagery of any sense mode involving a continuation of dream-like processes into the waking-up period. Confusions with real percepts commonly occur.

HYPNOSIS An altered mental state induced by hypnotism, and distinguished by unusual sensory, motor and memory phenomena. Such phenomena can closely resemble those that occur spontaneously in the hysterical neuroses (q.v.). Both have often been interpreted in terms of personality dissociation.

HYSTERIA (nothing to do with 'fits of hysterics'). A diagnostic category of neurosis in which physical symptoms like blindness, deafness, paralysis or amnesias occur, without an organic cause. MULTIPLE PERSONALITY is classified as one of the rarer forms of hysteria. Breuer and Freud's early work was on patients of this diagnostic group.

IMAGE A subjective experience relating to remembering, thinking or imagining, which reproduces or copies in part, with some degree of realism, a previous visual, auditory or other sensory experience. Nevertheless, images have a constructive as well as a merely reproductive aspect. This is most apparent in imagination images, and less evident, although still present, in memory images.

IMAGINARY COMPANION A phenomenon of childhood in which non-existent playmates (children and sometimes animals) have, for the child, a very real existence. Although they may be a nuisance within the household (e.g. needing to be 'fed') they are wholly compatible with good mental health. Occasionally imaginary companions persist into adult life. Some cases of MULTIPLE PERSONALITY involve sub-systems resembling imaginary companions.

IMAGINATION IMAGE A mental image whose origins in previous perception are difficult, or impossible, to trace. Such images are presumably products of composite earlier perceptual subject matter. Contrast MEMORY IMAGE.

LUCID DREAM A dream in which the sleeper knows he is dreaming and asleep. Contrast PRE-LUCID DREAM in which he is uncertain whether he is asleep or awake.

MEMORY IMAGE A mental image whose origins in previous perception can readily be traced.

MESCALINE A hallucinogenic drug which, like psilocybin and lysergic acid diethylamide, may produce upsurges of autonomous visual imagery, body-image disturbances, TIME DISCONTINUITIES and oddities of thinking. Its botanical origin is the peyote cactus of Mexico and New Mexico, but synthetic mescaline has ordinarily been used in recent experiments.

MULTIPLE PERSONALITY The existence (either as alternating personalities or through co-consciousness) of sub-systems of the personality, each personified and claiming a separate identity. (*Dual personality* when such sub-systems are confined to two only).

NEED Murray's term for motives as forces from within the organism, particularly motives which characterize one personality and help to distinguish it from others. Contrast PRESS as forces from the environment, and then contrast e.g. n. aggression and p. aggression (q.v.).

NEGATIVE HALLUCINATION Experiences in which a person is selectively imperceptive to aspects of the environment: e.g. Steinberg's nitrous oxide experiment, in which the subject ceased to perceive the table at which he was sitting.

OUT-OF-THE-BODY EXPERIENCES During sleep some people report the subjective impression that their DREAM BODY leaves their physical body. These experiences may also occur in the waking state. The term 'out-of-the-body experiences' is neutral between the naturalistic and supernatural interpretations placed upon the phenomenon.

PERSEVERATION The continuation of a psychological process without conscious control and even despite efforts to control it: e.g. the tune running through the head of a fatigued person, or that perseveration of a day's events which may accompany insomnia or provide subject-matter for a HYPNAGOGIC IMAGE.

PHOBIA An emotional habit involving an irrational feat of some object or situation: e.g. agoraphobia – fear of open spaces.

PRE-LUCID DREAM A dream in which the dreamer thinks he may be asleep and dreaming (contrast LUCID DREAM, in which he knows he is dreaming).

PRESS Forces which operate from the environment to evoke responses from the individual (Murray). Compare and contrast Murray's NEED for forces from within the personality itself.

PSYCHOLOGIST IN LITERATURE My term for a fictional character through whom an author expresses his understanding of psychological phenomena: e.g. some of Ibsen's characters, the Fool in *King Lear* and Dostoevsky's Ivan Karamazov.

RELATIVE ETHICS PRINCIPLE Shand's principle which states that each SENTIMENT tends to develop a relative ethics of its own: this permits moral exceptions *against* objects of negative sentiments and *for* objects of positive sentiments: e.g. with rivals in love, and enemies in war, we are freed from usual ethical restraints.

REMOTE VIEWING The alleged ability of some people to 'perceive' distant scenes and events in some clairvoyant way. Experiments which have sought to establish such 'remote viewing' have been found unconvincing; they appear to include clues unwittingly communicated to the subject in the instructions given.

REPRESSION Freud's term for forgetting, involving a passing out of consciousness of certain material as a result of strong motives not to remember. Repression should not be confused with dissociation, but it may sustain a dissociated system or contribute to its content.

SCHIZOPHRENIA (or better, the schizophrenias) Diagnostic term (Bleuler) for a group of major psychoses with no known cause, characterized by HALLUCINATION and frequently by delusion and thought disturbances. If dissociation is involved it is of a different kind from that of multiple personality: the personality of the schizophrenic is 'shattered' rather than 'split'.

SECONDARY PERCEPTION Perception which occurs not directly but through something intermediate, e.g. a picture, television, a film or other media. Secondary perception extends perception to the historically and geographically remote, and into the realm of the purely imaginary.

SENTIMENT An organized system of emotional dispositions centred around some object (Shand), e.g. loving and liking, or hating and disliking. It may be concrete particular (e.g. love of a particular person), concrete general (e.g. dislike of cats) or abstract (e.g. moral sentiments about 'right and wrong', 'good and evil', 'just and unjust').

SHADOW Jung's term for the negative, rejected and repressed aspects of the personality, as in Dr Jekyll's 'Mr Hyde' and Frankenstein's 'Monster'.

SOMNAMBULISM An episode which is simpler and briefer than a FUGUE in which a sub-system assumes control of the personality. Somnambulism is sometimes indentified with merely nocturnal somnambulism ('sleep walking'), but it may also occur during full wakefulness. In this case it tends to involve bizarre behaviour more likely to provoke attention than the fugue.

SUB-SYSTEM OF THE PERSONALITY An organization within the individual's mental life with some measure of autonomous functioning of its own. The larger sub-systems may involve changes of identity, as in MULTIPLE PERSONALITY; smaller sub-systems are evident in AUTOMATIC WRITING, AUTONOMOUS IMAGERY and post-hypnotic suggestions, and in emotional habits and motives.

SUGGESTION Inducing a person to accept a frame of reference without the intervention of his critical thought. There is evidence for different kinds of suggestion, e.g. sensory and motor.

Glossary

THOUGHT PRODUCTS A very general term I have used for socially useful productions of human thought, including novels and plays, paintings and other works of art, inventions and scientific theories. It is argued that two kinds of process play a part in their production: authorship processes (imagery and imagination) and editorship processes (evaluative critical thinking).

TIME DISCONTINUITIES Periods of amnesia, or ignorance of the passage of time. Events occurring in the amnesic periods may include events which are the causes of later events; the person concerned may thus have the impression of things suddenly occurring without apparent cause. Reported in FUGUES and MULTIPLE PERSONALITY cases.

UNDERMIND The term used by Enid Blyton for the sub-system outside her own consciousness which produced the upsurges of AUTONOMOUS IMAGERY which 'wrote her books for her'.

Bibliography

References to well-known works of literature have not been included. (In the case of Dostoevsky I have used the Constance Garnett translation.) There are other books, cited in the text by name, which have also been excluded from the following list. On occasions I have given two dates, the first indicating original publication when this seemed relevant and important.

ALEXANDER, U. K. A case study of multiple personality. *Journal of Abnormal and Social Psychology*, 1956, 52:2, 272–6.

ARDIS, J. A. and MCKELLAR, P. Hypnagogic imagery and mescaline. *Journal of Mental Sceince*, 1956, 102, 22–9.

ARIETI, S. *American handbook of psychiatry*. vol. 5. New York: Basic Books, 1975.

BARBER, T. X. Hypnosis, suggestion and auditory-visual 'hallucinations': a critical analysis. In W. KEUP (Ed.), *Origin and mechanisms of hallucinations*. New York, London: Plenum Press, 1970.

BARBER, T. X. *LSD, marihuana, yoga and hypnosis*. Chicago: Aldine Publishing Co., 1970.

BLEULER, E. *Textbook of psychiatry*. Publ 1916 (Trans. A. A. BRILL) New York: Macmillan, 1924.

BOURGUIGNON, E. (Ed.) *Religion, altered states of consciousness and social change*. Ohio State University Press, 1973.

BOWERS, K. S. Situtionism in psychology: an analysis and a critique. *Psychological Review*, 1973, 80, 307–36.

BREUER, J. and FREUD, S. *Studies on hysteria (1893–5)* Collected works of Freud. vol. 2 (Trans. J. STRACHEY). London: Hogarth.

BURT, C. *The young delinquent*. London: University of London 1937.

BUTLER, J. *Sermons on human nature*. 1729 (Ed. W. E. GLADSTONE). Oxford: Clarendon Press, 1897.

CLECKLEY, H. *The mask of sanity: an attempt to reinterpret the so-called psychopathic personality*. St Louis: Mosby, 1941.

CONWAY, D. *Magic: an occult primer*. London: Cape, 1972.

CUTLER, B. and REED, J. Multiple personality. *Psychological Medicine*, 1975, 5, 18–26.

DE COURMELLES, F. *Hypnotism*. (Trans. L. ENSOR). London: Routledge, 1891.

EKEHAMMAR, B. Interactionism in personality from a historical standpoint. *Psychological Bulletin*, 1974, 81:12, 1026–48.

ELLENBERGER, H. F. *The discovery of the unconscious*. Basic Books, 1970.

Bibliography

ELLENBERGER, H. F. The story of 'Anna O': and critical reviews of new data. *Journal of the History of Behavioural Sciences*, 1972, 8:3, 267–97.

ERIKSON, M. H. Experimental demonstrations of the psychopathology of everyday life. *Psychoanalytic Quarterly*, 1939, 8, 338–53.

EYSENCK, H. J., ARNOLD, W. and MEILI, R. (Eds) *Encyclopedia of Psychology*, vol. I, London: Search Press, 1972.

FODOR, N. *Encyclopaedia of Psychic Sciences*. New York: University Books, 1966.

FORTUNE, DION. *Psychic self-defence: a study in occult pathology and criminality*. 1930. London: Aquarian Press (Edition, 1963).

FREEMAN, A. M., KAPLAN, H. I. and SADOCK, B. J.)eds) *Comprehensive Textbook of Psychiatry*. Baltimore: Williams and Wilkins, 1975.

FREUD, S. 1900. *The interpretation of dreams*. (Trans. J. STRACHEY). London: Hogarth.

FREUD, S. 1909 The origin and development of psycho-analysis. In (Ed. J. RICKMAN). *A general selection from the works of Sigmund Freud*. London: Hogarth, 1937.

FREUD, S. 1923. *The ego and the id*. (Trans. J. STRACHEY). London: Hogarth. (*See also:* BREUER, J. and FREUD, S.).

GALTON, F. *The art of travel*. London: Murray, 1876.

GALTON, F. *Inquiries into human faculty and its development*. London: Macmillan, 1883.

GORDON, R. An investigation into some of the factors that favour the formation of stereotyped images. *British Journal of Psychology*, 1949, 39:3, 156–67.

GOSHEN, C. E. The original case material of psycho-analysis. *American Journal of Psychiatry*, 1951–52, 830–35.

GREEN, C. *Lucid dreams*. London: Hamilton, 1968.

GROSSMANN, L. *Dostoevsky: a biography*. (Trans. M. MACKIER). Published Moscow, 1962. London: Allen Lane, 1974.

HALE, N. G. (Ed.) *Morton Prince: psychotherapy and multiple personality selected essays*. Cambridge, Mass: Harvard University Press, 1975.

HARRIS, M. *Cows, pigs, wars and witches: the riddle of culture*. 1975.

HART, B. *The psychology of insanity*. 1912. Cambridge: University Press (Fifth edition 1957)

HART, B. *Psychopathology*. Cambridge: University Press, 1939.

HAYTER, A. *Opium and the romantic imagination*. London: Faber, 1968.

HILGARD, E. R. A neodissociation interpretation of pain reduction in hypnosis. *Psychological Review*, 1973, 80:5, 396–411.

HILGARD, E. R. Dissociation revisited. In M. HENLE, J. JAYNER and J. SULLIVAN (Eds) *Contributions to the history of psychology*. New York: Springer, 1973.

HILGARD, E. R. *Divided consciousness*. New York: Wiley, 1977.

HILGARD, E. R. and HILGARD, J. R. *Hypnosis and the relief of pain*. Los Altos, Kaufmann, 1975.

HOLT, E. B. *Animal drive and the learning process*. London: Williams and Norgate, 1931.

HUMPHREYS, C. *Buddhism*. Harmondsworth: Penguin Books, 1962.

HUNTER, I. M. L. *Memory*. Harmondsworth: Penguin Books, 1964.

JAENSCH, E. R. *Eidetic imagery*. London: Kegan Paul, 1930.

JAMES, W. *The principles of psychology*. London: Macmillan, 1890.

JANET, P. *The major symptoms of hysteria*. (1907) Second edition, New York: Macmillan, 1907.

JAYNES, J. *The origins of consciousness in the breakdown of the bicameral mind*. Boston: Houghton Mifflin, 1976.

JONES, E. *The life and work of Sigmund Freud*. New York: Basic Books, 1953.

KLÜVER, H. *Mescal and mechanisms of hallucination*. First published 1928. University of Chicago Press, 1966.

KOESTLER, A. *Arrow in the blue: an autobiography*. London: Collins and Hamilton, 1954.

LAIRD, J. *Problems of the self*. London: Macmillan, 1917.

LARMORE, K., LUDWIG, A. M. and CAIN, R. L. Multiple personality, an objective case study. *British Journal of Psychiatry*, 1977, 131, 35–40.

LEANING, F. E. An introductory study of hypnagogic phenomena. *Proceedings of the Society for Psychical Research*, 1925, 35, 289–403.

LOWES, J. L. *The road to Xanadu: a study in the ways of the imagination*. New York: Constable, 1927.

MCDOUGALL, W. *An outline of abnormal psychology* (1926). London: Methuen, 1933.

MCKELLAR, P. *A text-book of human psychology*. London: Cohen and West, 1952.

MCKELLAR, P. *Imagination and thinking*. New York: Basic Books, 1957.

MCKELLAR, P. The investigation of mental images. In S. A. BARNETT and A. MCLAREN, *Penguin Science Survey B* (Biological Sciences), Penguin Books, 1965, 79–94.

MCKELLAR, P. *Experience and behaviour*. Harmondsworth: Penguin Books, 1968.

MCKELLAR, P. Imagery from the standpoint of introspection. In P. W. SHEEHAN (Ed.), *The function and nature of imagery*. New York and London: Academic Press, 1972.

MCKELLAR, P. Twixt waking and sleeping. *Psychology Today* (European edition), 1975, 4, 20–4.

Bibliography

MCKELLAR, P. Autonomy, imagery and dissociation. *Journal of Mental Imagery*, 1977, 1, 93–108.

MCKELLAR, P. The Jekyll and Hyde in all of us. *Psychology Today* (European edition), 1977, 3:8.

MCKELLAR, P. The origins of violence. In *Violence, the community and the administrator.* Wellington: Institute of Public Administration, 1977.

MCKELLAR, P. and SIMPSON, L. Between wakefulness and sleep: hypnagogic imagery. *British Journal of Psychology*, 1954, 45, 266–76.

MCKELLAR, P. and TONN, H. Negative hallucination, dissociation and the five stamps experiment. *British Journal of Social Psychiatry*, 1967, 1:4, 260–70.

MARKS, D. and KAMANN, R. The non-psychic powers of Uri Geller. *The Zetetic*, 1977, 1:2, 9–17.

MARKS, D. and KAMMANN, R. Information transmission in remote viewing experiments. *Nature*, 1978, 274, 680–1.

MARX, O. M. Morton Prince and the dissociation of a personality. *Journal of the History of the Behavioural Sciences*, 1970, 6:2, 120–30.

MENNINGER, K. A. *The human mind.* (Third edition). New York: Knopf, 1946.

MORGAN, W. P. The mind of the marathon runner. *Psychology Today* (European edition), 1978, 4:6, 26–30.

MURRAY, H. *Explorations in personality.* Oxford University Press, 1938.

MURRAY, H. *Thematic apperception test,* and instruction manual. Harvard University Press, 1943.

MURRAY, H. Morton Prince: sketch of his life and work. *Journal of Abnormal Psychology*, 52, 1956, 291–5.

NAYRAE, P. Mental automatism. 1927. In (Ed.) S. R. HIRSCH *Themes and variations in European psychiatry: an anthology.* Bristol: Wright, 1974.

NEMIAH, J. C. Hysterical neurosis, dissociative type. In (Eds) A. M. FREEMAN, H. I. KAPLAN and B. J. SADOCK, *Comprehensive textbook of psychiatry* (2nd edition). Baltimore: Williams and Wilkins, 1975.

NORBU, D. *Red star over Tibet.* London: Collins, 1974.

PARRY, M. H. *Aggression on the road.* London: Tavistock, 1968.

PEAR, T. H. The relations of 'complex' and 'sentiment'. *British Journal of Psychology*, 1922, 13, 130–40.

PRINCE, M. The development and geneology of the Misses Beauchamp. (1901). In (Ed.) HALE, N. G., 1975, q.v.

PRINCE, M. *The dissociation of a personality.* London: Longmans, 1906.

PRINCE, M. *The unconscious.* New York: Macmillan, 1929.

RAWCLIFFE, D. H. *The psychology of the occult.* London: Ridgway, 1952.

RAWCLIFFE, D. H. *Illusions and delusions of the supernatural and the occult.* New York: Dover, 1959.

SARGANT, W. *The mind possessed.* London: Heinemann, 1973.

SCHACTER, D. L. The hypnagogic state: a critical review of the literature. *Psychological Bulletin,* 1976, 83:3, 452–81.

SCHREIBER, F. R. *Sybil: the true story of a woman possessed by sixteen separate personalities.* Harmondsworth: Penguin Books, 1975.

SEGAL, R. K. and WEST, L. J. *Hallucinations.* New York: Wiley, 1975.

SELIGMAN, K. *The history of magic.* New York: Pantheon, 1948.

SHAND, A. F. *Foundations of character.* London: Macmillan, 1914.

SHOR, R. E. and ORNE, M. T. The nature of hypnosis. New York: Holt, 1965.

SIEGEL, R. K. and WEST, L. J. (Eds) *Hallucinations: Behaviour, experience and theory.* New York: Wiley, 1975.

SILBERER, H. Report on a method of eliciting and observing certain symbolic hallucination phenomena, 1909. In D. RAPAPORT (Ed.) *Organization and pathology of thought.* New York: Columbia, 1951.

SIZEMORE, C. S. and PITILLO, E. S. *I'm Eve.* New York: Doubleday, 1977.

SKILTON, C. (Ed.) *The autobiography of Frank Richards.* (1952). Memorial edition, London: Skilton, 1962.

STEKEL, W. The polyphony of thought. 1924. In D. RAPAPORT (Ed.) *Organization and pathology of thought.* Columbia University, 1951.

STONE, G. P. and OLDENBURG, R. A. Wrestling. Chapter in (Eds) R. SLOVENKO and J. A. KNIGHT *Motivation in Play, Games and Sports.* Springfield, Illinois: Thomas, 1967.

STONEHOUSE, J. *My trial.* London: Wyndham, 1976.

STONEY, B. *Enid Blyton: a biography.* London: Hodder and Stoughton, 1974.

TART, C. T. *Altered states of consciousness.* New York: Wiley, 1969.

TAYLOR, W. S. and MARTIN, W. F. Multiple personality. *Journal of Abnormal and Social Psychology,* 1944, 39, 281–300.

THIGPEN, C. H. and CLECKLEY, H. A case of multiple personality. *Journal of Abnormal and Social Psychology,* 1954, 49, 135–51.

THOULESS, R. H. *An introduction to the psychology of religion.* Cambridge: University Press, 1928.

VAN DE CASTLE, R. L. Anthropology and psychic research. In E. D. MITCHELL (Ed.), *Psychic exploration.* New York: Putnam, 1974.

VAN EEDEN, F. A study of dreams, 1913. Chapter 8 in (Ed.) C. T. TART, *Altered States of Consciousness.* New York: Wiley, 1969.

WATSON, J. B. *Psychology from the standpoint of a behaviourist.* Philadelphia: Lippincott, 1919.

YELLOWLEES, H. *Clinical lectures on psychological medicine.* London: Churchill, 1932.

Index

Index